SEYMOUR

Let Freedom Ring

A History of the Jews in the United States

Melyssa Nadow

BEHRMAN HOUSE, INC.

PROJECT EDITOR
Ruby G. Strauss

BOOK AND COVER DESIGN
Pronto Design & Production, Inc.

PHOTO CREDITS
Photo Researcher: Lynn Goldberg Biderman

The editor and publisher gratefully acknowledge the cooperation of the following sources of photographs for this book:

Comstock, Inc.: Cover; Bettmann: 9 (top), 10 (top), 10 (bottom), 15 (top), 18 (top), 26 (bottom), 29 (bottom), 35 (top), 38 (top right), 38 (bottom), 43 (right), 44 (bottom), 59, 67, 73 (middle), 76 (top), 76 (bottom), 78 (top), 78 (middle), 85, 86, 87, 93; The Jewish Museum: 9 (bottom); 18 (bottom); 20 (top), 25 (bottom), 27, 30 (bottom), 39, 40, 41 (top), 41 (bottom); American Jewish Archives: 11, 17, 21 (bottom), 23 (bottom), 29 (middle), 30 (top), 31 (bottom), 38 (top left), 59, 61, 78 (bottom), 82 (bottom right); Museum of the City of New York: The J. Clarence Davies Collection 12 (top), 43 (top), 44 (top); The New-York Historical Society: 12 (bottom); Biblioteque Nationale: 13; The Society of Friends of Touro Synagogue 16; American Jewish Historical Society: 19, 20 (bottom), 21 (top), 24, 25 (top), 26 (top), 28 (bottom), 32, 47, 65 (top), 72; Museum of American Jewish History: 20 (middle); HUC/JIR: 22, 23 (top); 90 (top and bottom); Library of Congress: 28 (top), 34 (top and bottom); Minnesota Historical Society: 29 (top); Historical Society of Southern Florida: 31 (top); Smithsonian Institution: 33, 64; National Council of Jewish Women: 42 (top); YIVO: 42 (bottom); American Jewish Committee: 48; Jewish Theological Seminary/Joyce Culver 46 (bottom), 91 (top); Bill Aron Photography: 50, 51; Lou Malkin: 52; International Ladies Garment Workers Union Archives: 53 (top), 54 (bottom), 55 (bottom), 57, 58; Amalgamated Clothing and Textile Workers Union: 55 (top), 56; Rutgers News Service: 62 (bottom right); Fred Stein: 62 (top); National Foundation: 62 (bottom left); FPG International: 66 (bottom), 77 (top and bottom); Albert Einstein Medical Center: 66 (top); Eric Pollitzer: 68; Bildarchiv Preussischer Kulture Besitz: 69; Keystone Press: 70 (bottom); State of Israel Government Press Office: 73 (top); United States Holocaust Memorial Museum: 74; The American Battle Monuments Commission: 75; Joint Distribution Committee: 80 (top); Israeli Consulate: 83; United Nations: 84 (bottom); Francene Keery: 91 (bottom).

Published by
BEHRMAN HOUSE, INC.
235 Watchung Avenue, West Orange, New Jersey 07052

ISBN: 0-87441-582-9
Manufactured in the United States of America

For Sheldon Zimmerman

He sees a generation eager for Torah and teaches it at every turn, as it is said,
"There is that which is given away and is yet increased" (*B. Berachot 63a*).

—*SR*

*I lift my lamp beside
the golden door!*

—Emma Lazarus,
"The New Colossus," 1883

C O N T E N T S

Introduction

You don't have to live too many years before discovering that history can be fun. If you are a tennis or baseball fan, you probably recall last year's championship game, or remember who was the winner the year before that. You may have memorized dozens of facts about tennis matches or the World Series. You may not think of this as history, but it is.

Or you may see a television program about a famous person—maybe a movie star, a president, or a poet—and say to yourself, "I'd like to know more about that person." Soon you might know lots of stories about Barbra Streisand, John F. Kennedy, or Emily Dickinson. You may not think of this as history, but it is.

Even wondering about yourself is history. You might wonder: Who was at my first birthday party? How much did I weigh when I was born? Or, looking at a photograph in your family album, you might ask about the foreign-looking man with the whiskers. And if you discover that you are looking at your great-great grandfather when he was a young man, you might ask: What kind of work did he do? Was he the first in our family to come to America?

Actually, it would be strange if you were not interested in history. After all, you make history every day of your life. Many years from now someone will find a videotape of you smiling into the camera, and that person will wonder what your life was all about. And someone who remembers you will say: "That was one of our relatives a long time ago. You can't imagine what an interesting life that person led! Let me tell you about it." Wouldn't it be fascinating to be able to turn the clock forward and hear about your life and how you lived it? You would be eavesdropping on someone teaching history.

When you hear how Steven Spielberg began directing movies, how Harry Houdini became a world-famous magician, and how Golda Meir became the first woman prime minister of the State of Israel, you are simply turning the clock backward for a moment. Turning the clock backward gives you a chance to see how other people lived their lives.

We are going to turn the clock back. Not very far back—just a few hundred years. Just far enough to explain a lot of things about how we live in America today. You are going to read some of our best stories—stories about Jews who came to America, stories about Jews who were born in America and grew up to change the America they were born in, and stories about Jews who made your life what it is now.

America's Jews have always been few in number, yet they managed to do great and marvelous things. They used their intelligence and imagination just as other Americans did. But more than that, in every generation they brought Jewish values and ideals into American life. You can share the pride in their achievements, and in your own generation perhaps you can even achieve new greatness that the rest of us can share.

We'll begin with the story of the first Jews to come to America.

| 1492 | Columbus sails from Spain. | 1620 | The Pilgrims land at Plymouth Rock. | 1654 | The first Jewish settlers arrive in New Amsterdam. |

Also in this chapter: The year the first rabbi came to the New World. *What was his name?*

The First Jews in America

The story of the Jews in America begins in Spain, just before America was discovered. In 1478 King Ferdinand set up the Inquisition to seek out people who said they had converted to the Catholic faith, but secretly practiced other religions. These included many of the Jews in Spain.

For fourteen years the Inquisition used torture and death as its weapons against Jews who had only pretended to become Catholics. These were the "crypto" or "secret" Jews. They were often helped by Jews who had refused to convert. Finally, on March 31, 1492, the king ordered all Jews in Spain to convert to Catholicism or leave the country by July 31.

Conversos was the name given to Jews who converted to the Catholic faith. Those called crypto **Jews only pretended to convert, while secretly continuing to practice Judaism.**

The first Jew to set foot in America arrived in that same year. His name was Luis de Torres, and he was a *converso*—he was born a Jew, but converted to Catholicism just before sailing away from Spain. History might have forgotten all about him, except that he sailed with one of the most important explorers of all time.

When Christopher Columbus was getting ready for his famous voyage in search of a new passage to the Far East, he needed an interpreter. He chose Luis de Torres. It was a good choice. Luis de Torres knew Hebrew and Spanish as well as Aramaic and some Arabic. Knowing that all Jews—even those who had only pretended to convert—would soon be forced to leave Spain, the opportunity to sail with Columbus came just at the right moment for Luis de Torres.

▲ During your first history lessons you probably learned the names of Columbus' three ships (pictured above). Did you know that at least six members of the crew came from families that were once Jewish?

◄ Between 1481 and 1492 some 13,000 Jews were put to death by the Inquisition, often in public burnings like the one shown in this drawing.

▲ *Using the "Jacob's staff,"* or quadrant invented by Levi ben Gershom, ships' navigators could calculate their location during daylight hours.

▲ *The astrolabe, an instrument* used by Jewish astrologers, allowed sailors to navigate at night by measuring the position of the planets.

How the Jews Helped Columbus

Columbus received advice and help from Jewish experts and scientists. He talked about geography with the best mapmaker of the age, Judah Cresques. He plotted the course of his ships using the writings of the Jewish astronomer Abraham Zacuto. And on his three ships Columbus had the help of at least five *conversos*, including his surgeon, the fleet physician, and Luis de Torres, his interpreter.

You may have heard how Queen Isabella gave Columbus some of her jewels to buy the ships and supplies required for the journey. Yet much more money was needed, and it came from ordinary people—merchants and investors. Among these were a number of *conversos*, including another Luis—Luis de Santangel. Luis de Santangel was the chancellor of Spain, the country's most important money-manager. Not only did he convince Queen Isabella to support Columbus' exploration, he also made an additional large personal loan to the explorer. In these ways, the Jews of Spain played an important part in the discovery of America.

The First Jew in the New World

Columbus and his crew set sail on August 3, 1492. The three ships—the *Nina*, the *Pinta*, and the *Santa Maria*—reached land on October 12 of the same year.

Columbus "discovered" what Europeans called a New World. **It was not called America until 1507, when it was named for the explorer Amerigo Vespucci.**

Columbus first landed on a small island in the Bahamas and then on the island now called Cuba. He was disappointed with his explorations and returned to Spain. But Luis de Torres decided to remain. He had made friends with the natives and learned their language, and one of the chiefs gave him some land.

History has all but forgotten Luis de Torres, but he was one of the first Europeans in America, and certainly the first who had been born a Jew. Was he also the first Jew to find religious freedom in America? We can only wonder whether Luis de Torres, free of Spain and the Inquisition, continued to be a Catholic or returned to his Jewish faith.

Some historians say that Luis de Torres gave Columbus a letter to deliver to his relatives in Spain. He invited other Spanish Jews to join him in the "new" world. That letter was written 500 years ago. *If you were to write a letter to Jews in Spain today telling them why you think America is a good place to live now, what would you say?*

The First Jewish Settlement

By the early 1500s, soon after Columbus' voyage, groups of Spanish and Portuguese Jewish *conversos* were making the long and difficult sea voyage to the New World. They settled in Brazil, managing farms and producing sugar. Some even grew wealthy.

Under Dutch rule, the Jews in Brazil were allowed to worship in freedom. They built a synagogue and ran two Jewish schools in the city of Recife. But when the Portuguese conquered the city in 1654, the Jews were given the same choice they had faced before: death or exile.

Northward

Most of the 150 Jewish families decided to leave Brazil. Many headed back to Holland. Some boarded a ship named the *Valk* bound for islands in the Caribbean Sea. The Spanish in charge of those islands refused to allow the Jews to stay. So they boarded a French ship, the *Ste. Catherine*, bound for the Dutch port in North America—New Amsterdam. Before their departure they sent letters to their friends back in Holland, asking for money to be sent to New Amsterdam, but the letters took longer to get to Holland than the Jews took to get to New Amsterdam.

Isaac Aboab da Fonseca ▶

was the first rabbi in the New World. He arrived in Recife in 1642, but when the Portuguese recaptured the city, he was among the Jews who returned to Holland.

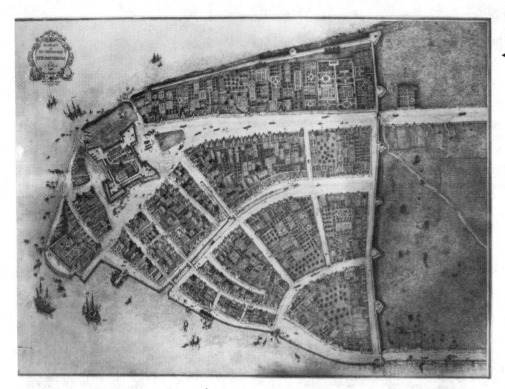

◀ *The city of New York started as a small Dutch town on the tip of an island. In 1626 Peter Minuit, working for the Dutch West India Company, purchased the island from the Manhattan Indians for a few dollars' worth of beads, blankets, and trinkets. This map shows New Amsterdam in 1660, five years after the Jews were given permission to settle in the colony.*

▲ *Peter Stuyvesant disliked all "strangers" who arrived in New Amsterdam. From the beginning, the Jewish battle for religious freedom in North America became a struggle for the rights of all minorities.*

The First Jewish Community in North America

So it happened that after six months at sea, twenty-three penniless Jews came ashore in New Amsterdam, the city that would one day be New York. The captain of the *Ste. Catherine* immediately took his case against the Jews to the court. He told the judge that he was owed 1,567 guilders.✪ The Jews explained that they would gladly pay this remaining fare as soon as they received money from their relatives and friends in Holland. Instead, the court ordered that the personal property they owned be sold at auction. But they had so little that the sale brought hardly any money at all. Some of the Jews were placed in jail as hostages until the full debt could be paid.

The whole matter came to the attention of a very famous man, Governor Peter Stuyvesant. Stuyvesant wrote home to his employers, the directors of the Dutch West India Company, asking for permission to force all the Jews to leave New Amsterdam.

✪ A **guilder** was a gold coin from the Netherlands.

I t is a wonder of our history that in times of trouble there are often Jews in another part of the world who are ready and able to help. *Can you describe recent examples of this?*

Dutch Jews worship in the Amsterdam synagogue in Holland.

When the directors of the Dutch West India Company gave permission for the Jews to settle in New Amsterdam, there were three reasons for their decision. The Jews had shown their loyalty to Holland by defending the Brazilian colony of Recife, and they had promised that other Jewish colonists would come. The third reason may surprise you: Jews in Holland owned a large part of the Dutch West India Company!

Back in Holland friends of the New Amsterdam Jews also wrote to the Dutch West India Company, reminding the directors that these Jews had fought to defend the Dutch city of Recife against the Portuguese. They reminded the directors that the New Amsterdam Jews had always been loyal citizens of the Dutch colony. In addition, they promised to encourage other Jews to come and settle in New Amsterdam to help the colony grow.

In the spring a ship arrived from Holland bringing money and provisions. It also brought permission for the Jews to remain in New Amsterdam provided that "the poor among them shall not become a burden . . . but be supported by their own people."

Asser Levy was most probably among the original twenty-three Jews in New Amsterdam. Within ten years of his arrival, Levy became one of the wealthiest men in the colonies. He traded in furs, bought real estate, and owned and operated the first butcher shop in the New World, where he refused to slaughter hogs.

When the Lutherans of New Amsterdam needed money to construct their first church, Levy lent them the funds. His reputation as a prosperous and generous man was widespread in America.

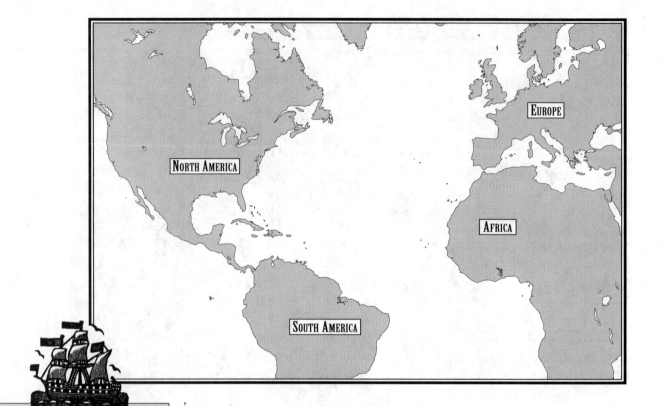

Plot the Course

Find the following routes on the map:

⬥ In 1492 Columbus sailed from Spain to Cuba.

⬥ In the early 1500s Portuguese Jews journeyed to Brazil.

⬥ Jews from Brazil were taken to New Amsterdam in 1654.

⬥ A ship traveling from Holland to New Amsterdam brought permission for the Jews to remain in the colony.

The Early Struggle for Jewish Rights

The first battle for religious liberty in America had been won. But this was not by any means the end of the struggle. Within the next few years the Jews continued to seek one freedom after another. They received the right not to appear in court on Saturday. They received land for a Jewish cemetery. Slowly they gained rights to engage in free trade, to serve in local guard units, to own real estate, and finally, to become full citizens of the colony.

Looking Ahead

By the time of the American Revolution fewer than 3,000 Jews had settled among the 2.5 million people in the thirteen colonies. And in each colony they struggled for equal rights.

The next chapter describes Jewish life in North America before the Revolution. The word was spreading to Jews in Europe: America was a place Jews might go to find freedom.

2 A New World with Old Values

▲ *The Thanksgiving holiday in America was patterned after the Jewish festival of Sukkot.*

The Jews had found a new home in a land where they could live according to Jewish traditions. The colonies were ruled by laws taken from the Christian Old Testament, which is the Hebrew Bible. Ministers often quoted their Old Testament in their sermons and many believed that they were the true "New Jews." Christians in New England observed their Sunday Sabbath strictly, adopting many customs that Jews had followed for centuries, such as closing their places of business and studying the Bible during worship services. Many democratic features of colonial life, such as town meetings, were based on readings in the Hebrew Bible.

The Jews were recognized as the "People of the Book"—members of the religious group that had given the Bible to the world. While this did not bring special treatment to Jews living in the colonies, in most places they were allowed to live comfortably as Jews.

◀ *The Liberty Bell in Philadelphia was cast twenty-five years before the American Revolution. It is inscribed with words from the Hebrew Bible: "Proclaim liberty throughout all the land unto all the inhabitants thereof." (Leviticus 25:10)*

The First Synagogues

The British armies conquered New Amsterdam from the Dutch in 1664 and renamed it New York. The British soon gave the Jews more freedom, permitting them to build a synagogue. Construction on the first synagogue in North America, Shearith Israel, was begun in 1728.

Has the role of the synagogue in Jewish life changed since colonial times? In what ways? In what ways does it remain the same?

Jewish life was centered almost entirely on the synagogue. The synagogue cared for the Jewish cemetery, supervised the kosher butcher, made sure that bakers produced enough matzah for Passover, and educated Jewish children. There were no public schools, so the synagogue school taught English, Spanish, and arithmetic in addition to religious subjects.

Not far away the colony of Rhode Island had been founded in 1636 by Roger Williams, a young minister. Williams had left Massachusetts and founded Rhode Island so that all people could have a place to worship in freedom. By the 1740s many Jews had settled in Newport, Rhode Island, and had established a synagogue there.

How old is your synagogue? • Did your congregation ever meet in a different building? • Where? • Does your synagogue have a cemetery? • Where? • How many people belong to your synagogue? • How many students attend your religious school?

The first synagogue in the colonies was on Mill Street in New Amsterdam, which is now known as South William Street in Manhattan's financial district.

In Newport, Rhode Island, ▶
Yeshuat Yisrael, now known as the Touro Synagogue, was completed in 1763. The oldest remaining synagogue building in the United States, it can still be visited today.

International Traders

The Jews of North America settled in seaports such as New York and Newport, Philadelphia and Charleston. International trade took place at these port cities, and trade was a good business for many of America's Jews.

There were two reasons for this. First, American Jews had contacts with other Jews throughout the world—family and friends—on whom they could depend. Second, because they shared the same religious laws, the Jews of North America could rely on Jews in distant Europe to be honest in their business dealings.

The First Ashkenazic Jews Arrive

Nearly all of the early Jewish settlers during colonial times came from southern Europe, North Africa, and Asia. They had Spanish and Portuguese backgrounds and were known as Sephardim.°

By 1700 the great emigration of Sephardim had ended. A newer wave of Jewish immigrants came to America from northern Europe—from Holland, England, and Germany. They were called Ashkenazim.° By the 1730s the number of Ashkenazim in America was greater than the number of Sephardim.

° **Sephardim** comes from the Hebrew name for Spain, Sepharad.

° **Ashkenazim** is a word derived from the Hebrew name for France and Germany, Ashkenaz.

▲ *Charles Town (now Charleston), South Carolina, became the greatest Southern seaport in colonial America. Its Jewish community included merchants and shipowners.*

The hero of the Revolution was George Washington (shown in the winter of 1777-1778 at Valley Forge). When he became president, he championed the cause of liberty for all. Years later, President Washington wrote to the Jews of Newport, Rhode Island, saying, "May the children of the stock of Abraham who dwell in this land continue to merit and enjoy the good will of the other inhabitants. . . All possess alike liberty of conscience and immunities of citizenship."

▲ *One design proposed in 1782 for the official seal of the United States showed the splitting of the Sea of Reeds and the escape of the Children of Israel from the pursuing Egyptian army. The biblical story of the Exodus has inspired movements for the liberation of oppressed peoples throughout history.*

The Revolution

Serious disagreements were developing between the colonies and the British government. The colonists were not allowed to be elected to the British Parliament in London; nonetheless, the Parliament demanded that the colonists pay taxes. Finally, in April 1775, the thirteen colonies revolted against the British. The American Revolution had begun.

Like other Americans, the Jews in the colonies were divided on the issue of revolution. Some remained loyal to the British government: Under British rule their life in America was better than it had been in Europe; they were allowed to settle in most of the colonies, to worship freely, and to participate in the prosperous colonial trade. Other Jews favored revolution: The British taxes on trade and the restrictions on imports threatened their businesses. Some 100 Jews fought in the Continental Army under George Washington. But the most famous Jew of Revolutionary times was no soldier. His name was Haym Salomon.

HAYM SALOMON

Unlike most Polish Jews of his time, Haym Salomon loved to travel. In his younger years he visited one Jewish community after another in northern Europe. As he wandered, Salomon began to dream of going to the New World. Finally, in about 1772, he came to New York. At the start of the Revolution he was captured by the British and accused of being a spy (which he was). The British imprisoned and tortured him, but his wife and friends helped him escape. He fled to Philadelphia, where he sold bonds, lent money, and became broker to the Office of Finance.

What did a broker do? During the Revolutionary War money was scarce. People often paid their taxes in the form of farm products and animal hides. Haym Salomon would sell this merchandise for cash. In addition, Salomon made loans to some of the leaders of the new republic and contributed much of his fortune to the new government. Some government leaders avoided taking loans from Salomon, for it was said that he never asked to be repaid.

Many years later a statue was erected in Chicago showing George Washington clasping the hands of the treasurer, Robert Morris, and the broker Haym Salomon, celebrating the part that finance played in gaining the freedom of the new nation.

Haym Salomon worked hard for the new government. He contributed nearly all of his financial resources to help the cause of freedom. *What cause is very important to you? Why? • What do you do to support it?*

ROBERT MORRIS · GEORGE WASHINGTON · HAYM SALOMON
★ ★ ★
THE GOVERNMENT OF THE UNITED STATES
WHICH GIVES TO BIGOTRY NO SANCTION TO PERSECUTION
NO ASSISTANCE REQUIRES ONLY THAT THEY WHO LIVE UNDER
ITS PROTECTION SHOULD DEMEAN THEMSELVES AS GOOD CITIZENS
IN GIVING IT ON ALL OCCASIONS THEIR EFFECTUAL SUPPORT
PRESIDENT GEORGE WASHINGTON 1790
★ ★ ★

While few of the early Jewish settlers in America converted to Christianity, many did marry non-Jews. *Can you explain why this might have been so?*

A successful merchant with a fleet of thirty ships, Aaron Lopez was an observant Jew and did not conduct business on the Sabbath. During the Revolutionary War his home and warehouse were confiscated by the British because he supported the patriots.

Rebecca Gratz devoted her life to charity and was a tireless worker and fund-raiser for the Orphan Society, the Hebrew Sunday School Society, and other Philadelphia communal associations that she founded.

Gershom Mendes Seixas, was the first American-born religious leader of a Jewish congregation. His sermons called for funds to help starving Indians and those left homeless by the British in the War of 1812. He was also an educational leader, elected to the first Board of Regents for the State University of New York.

Looking Ahead

When the Revolutionary War ended, freedom of religion became the national policy of the new United States. A large wave of immigrants would soon come to America, having heard that America was a land of opportunity—a place where they could build a better life for themselves and for their children. America was also a place where they could worship freely.

The next chapter tells how Judaism changed in America, even as the issue of slavery almost split the nation in two.

| 1800 | Jews begin arriving in large numbers from Germany. | 1861 | The Civil War begins. | 1875 | Hebrew Union College is founded. |

Also in this chapter: The year a monthly Jewish magazine was printed in America. *What was its name?*

3 Religion, Slavery, and War

In the 1800s Jews began to arrive in America in large numbers. They came from central Europe, especially Germany, in search of economic opportunity and safety.

From 1840 to 1869 the Jewish population of the United States rose from 15,000 to 150,000.

Unlike earlier immigrants, the German Jews did not settle in the port cities. Instead, they moved westward as the frontier moved, to places such as Cincinnati, Pittsburgh, St. Louis, and New Orleans. In Michigan, Jewish families settled in Ann Arbor, Detroit, and Grand Rapids. By 1860 there were at least 1,500 Jews living in Chicago.

Wherever they settled, the German Jews established synagogues. And as the number of Jews in a town grew, the number of synagogues also increased.

◄ *German Jewish immigrants, such as the Baer brothers in Arkansas, established stores in the West.*

◄ *Construction of the first synagogue in the Mississippi Valley, St. Louis' Congregation B'nai El, was begun in 1885.*

America was a free country. In a democracy individuals have the right to make up their own minds, to choose what is right for them. This freedom carried over into synagogue life. The synagogues in America were traditional, yet each of them practiced a slightly different flavor of Judaism. Each congregation had its own leadership and each synagogue treasured its own independence.

Wise and the Reform Movement

Isaac Mayer Wise was the most important American rabbi of his time. He came to America in 1846, before the Jews of Germany began to pour into the United States.

Wise was convinced that America needed a new kind of Judaism. He saw a bright future for America's Jews if only they could unite to reform Judaism in a way that would fit America, just as some rabbis in Germany and Austria were then reforming Judaism. Unlike more traditional Jews, Wise felt it was necessary to change Jewish laws—to relax the laws of *kashrut*, to allow Jews to work on Saturday, and to make more use of English in prayers.

In addition to wanting reforms, Wise also believed that America's congregations should be united in a union, just as the new states of America were united. He issued a new prayerbook for his Cincinnati congregation, calling it *Minhag America* ("The American Ritual"), hoping it would be adopted by all American synagogues. When the Union of American Hebrew Congregations was formed in 1873, Wise began work on his next dream, a school to train American rabbis. In 1875 he opened the Hebrew Union College in Cincinnati. As president of the college he ordained more than sixty rabbis. In 1889 he became president of the Central Conference of American Rabbis, the association of Reform rabbis that he helped to found.

The synagogue in Charleston, South Carolina, issued a resolution saying that any attempt to unify the synagogues was unfitting to "the spirit of American Liberty."

Rabbi Isaac Mayer Wise founded Reform Judaism ▶
in America. Rabbi Wise began his career in Europe, but it was not until he reached America that he showed himself as a great reformer. In America, he worked for changes in Jewish law, unity among American Jewish synagogues, and the training and education of American-born rabbis. What was it about America in those pioneering days that might have caused this change in Rabbi Wise? Did living in Cincinnati, which was then on the Western frontier, change his thinking?

▲ *The Hebrew Union College in Cincinnati, Ohio, founded in 1875 by Rabbi Isaac Mayer Wise, is the oldest rabbinical school in the United States.*

Where are rabbis trained today?

Reform:
Hebrew Union College-Jewish Institute of Religion

Conservative:
The Jewish Theological Seminary of America

Orthodox:
Yeshiva University

Reconstructionist:
The Reconstructionist Rabbinical College

At which school did your rabbi study?

Tradition and Change

Reform Judaism taught that Jews should be more concerned with the way people behave toward one another than with rituals like *kashrut* and Sabbath observance. To some American Jews this idea seemed natural in a land of freedom like America. Reform Judaism seemed to be able to change to fit the way American Jews lived and worked.

While other Jews accepted the need to update Jewish law and practice, they felt that the Reform movement was making too many changes to the tradition. They attempted to make minor changes in Jewish ritual while "conserving" Jewish customs and ceremonies.

Before there was a Conservative movement, traditional Jews like Isaac Leeser of Philadelphia were already beginning to think in this new way. Leeser translated the Hebrew Bible into English and made English sermons a feature of the Sabbath morning service. His work was continued by Rabbis Benjamin Szold, Sabato Morais, and Alexander Kohut. In 1886 they founded the Jewish Theological Seminary to train "traditional" rabbis.

THE OCCIDENT,
AND
AMERICAN JEWISH ADVOCATE.

| Vol. I.] | NISSAN 5603, APRIL 1843. | [No. 1. |

INTRODUCTORY REMARKS.

It is a time-honoured custom, that when an Editor appears for the first time before the public, he is to state something of the course he means to pursue, and of the subjects he intends laying before his readers. In our case, this is hardly necessary, since the name of "Jewish Advocate" amply shadows forth that we mean to devote our pages to the spread of whatever can advance the cause of our religion, and of promoting the true interest of that people which has made this religion its profession ever since the days of the great lawgiver, through whom it was handed down to the nation descended from the stock of Abraham. But this general view may, perhaps, not be sufficiently detailed for many whom we would gladly number among our readers; and we will therefore briefly state our object in assuming the editorship of this new periodical, and of the course it is our firm determination to pursue.

With regard to our object, we state candidly, that the plan of a religious periodical did not originate with ourself, nor did we approve of it when it was first suggested to us. We thought then and still think, that newspaper knowledge is at best but superficial or, to make a paper or magazine really interesting to the general public, (and for such a one it is our duty to labour in our present vocation,) much matter must be admitted which is more pleasing in its nature than instructive, and the variety, which is to be constantly furnished, will naturally prevent long and continuous articles being given, although they might be extremely rich in information, even such as the people stand most in need of. We dreaded, moreover, that despite of the greatest care which we could bestow, articles might at times gain admission which

VOL. I.   1

◄ *Isaac Leeser founded a monthly Jewish magazine. This is part of the first page. What was the name of Leeser's magazine? In what year was it published?*

◀ *Some Jewish families were divided by the Civil War — brother fought against brother. This photograph shows Major Charles H. Jonas, a Confederate soldier who was captured by the Union troops. His brother Edward was an officer in the Illinois regiment of the Union army.*

T. J. Heffernam, A, 163 N. Y., hip and arm.
Serg. F. Herrfnkneckt, 7 " head.
M. Ellis, 23 N. J., hand.
Moses Steinburg, 142 Penn., legs bruised.
A. Newman, A, 72 " ankle
Lt. H. T. Davis, 81 " arm.
J. Killenbeck, 4 N. J., head.
S. S. Vanuess, 15 " leg.
W. Truax, 23 " back.
J. Hirsh, 4 " "
Jacob Schmidt, 19 Penn., left arm.
Jos. Osback, 19 " wounded.
W. Jabob, 19 " left arm.
Lieut. Simpson, 19 " left leg.
Capt. Schub, 19 " wounded.
C. M. Phillips, 16 Maine, cheek.
Lieut. S. Simpson, 99 Penn., leg.
R. Harris, 107 " thigh.
L. Brauer, wounded.
—— Wolf, 5 Penn., side.
R. Ellis, 2 " leg (slight).
S. Davidson, 186 " foot.
A. Valanstein, 105 N. Y., leg.
H. Stottler, 136 Penn., leg.

▲ *This partial list of Jews wounded at the Battle of Fredericksburg was published in 1862 in* The Jewish Record, *a New York newspaper.*

The Civil War

As the nation grew in size, the issue of slavery took on great importance. New states were being formed. Should they be slave or free? When Abraham Lincoln was elected president, he declared that the nation could not live "half slave and half free." The Southern states took this statement as an attack on their way of life, and they broke away from the North in 1861. Lincoln refused to allow the Union to dissolve into two nations. The Civil War had begun.

Nearly 7,000 Jews fought for the Union during the Civil War. Another 3,000 served in the Confederate army.

The war divided Jews just as it divided all Americans. In the North and in many of the border states Jews worked to abolish slavery completely. But just as Jews in the North were loyal to the Union, Jews in the South proved loyal to the Confederacy. Some of the Southern Jews were slaveholders. Many Southern Jews pointed to the Bible as permitting the ownership of slaves.

JUDAH P. BENJAMIN

The best-known Jew of the Civil War period was Judah P. Benjamin. He was a successful Louisiana lawyer and part owner of a sugar plantation. He entered politics and was elected to the Louisiana state assembly. In 1852 Benjamin's sugar crop was ruined by floods, and he was forced to sell his plantation and slaves. In that same year he was elected U.S. senator for Louisiana.

He was an outstanding senator, and President Millard Fillmore offered him a seat on the Supreme Court of the United States, but Benjamin decided to stay in politics instead. When the Southern states seceded from the Union in 1861, Benjamin resigned from the Senate. He served as the Confederacy's secretary of war and then as its secretary of state. With the Confederacy facing defeat in 1865, Benjamin fled to England, where he became one of England's most respected lawyers.

Can you see whose picture is on this Confederate two-dollar bill?

▲ *Rabbi Jacob Frankel was the first Jewish chaplain appointed by Abraham Lincoln.*

In 1861 the U.S. Congress passed a law stating that each regiment of the Union army should have a chaplain✤ "of some Christian denomination." Northern Jews wrote to President Lincoln, to the Senate, and to the House of Representatives, seeking the right of rabbis to serve as chaplains alongside priests and ministers. President Lincoln agreed, and by 1862 the law was changed to include rabbis. Three rabbis served as chaplains during the Civil War.

✤ *A chaplain is a member of the clergy officially attached to the armed forces to serve the religious needs of military personnel.*

Ernestine Rose

The Queen of Platforms

One of the most interesting Jews of the Civil War period was Ernestine Rose. While many women were content to marry, raise children, and continue to teach Judaism to the next generation, Ernestine Rose spoke out publicly on issues like slavery and the rights of women. In New York she was known as the "Queen of Platforms," and her speeches were well-attended. Around 1850 she began to seek voting rights for all the women of America.

During the Civil War, Ernestine Rose and many other well-known women collected signatures on a petition supporting President Lincoln's Emancipation Proclamation. After the Civil War she opposed the Fourteenth and Fifteenth Amendments to the Constitution, which emancipated blacks, because they did not also emancipate women. In 1869 she helped found the Women's Suffrage✿ Society, which continued to work for the rights of American women.

Healing the Wounds

The Civil War period brought many memories of European anti-Semitism to America's Jews. When the war was going badly in the North, General Ulysses S. Grant accused the Jews of using the war to make large profits for themselves. Abraham Lincoln quickly accused General Grant of treating Jews unfairly.

In the same way, when the war was going badly for the South, many southerners blamed local Jewish merchants for high prices and supply shortages. And so, the American Jewish community on both sides experienced similar outbreaks of anti-Semitic feelings.

More important, America's Jews understood the importance of helping their sisters and brothers in need. Despite the deep wounds caused by the war, the practice of helping one another continued to be the hallmark of Jewish life in America.

✿ **Suffrage** *is the right or privilege to vote. The Constitution of the United States originally gave this right only to men.*

In 1920 the Nineteenth Amendment to the Constitution guaranteed women in the United States the right to vote. *What rights do women continue to fight for in America today?*

Thus in 1865, following the Civil War, Jews in New York and Philadelphia sent thousands of pounds of matzah to Savannah so that the Jews of Georgia could celebrate the Passover holiday. Jewish traders in the North increased their business with Jewish traders in the South to help them get back on their feet.

▲ *This Purim ball took place in New York City in 1865 to raise funds to help Civil War orphans and widows.*

Looking Ahead

From 1840 to 1880 the Jews were still a tiny minority of the American population. Most owned small businesses, some were doctors and lawyers, a few had reached high office in government. As the South struggled to rebuild, new businesses were established. This was also a period of rapid growth in the North and in the West. What was everyday life like for America's Jews in the 1800s?

Also in this chapter: The year an important department store was founded. *What was its name?*

4 Jewish Life in the 1800s

Jewish peddlers brought necessary household goods to isolated frontier homes.

American Jews were on the move, all across the continent. As pioneers began the westward movement that would spread the United States to the Pacific Ocean, the Jews joined them. Many of these were German Jewish peddlers who later became merchants and store owners.

Of course, some of the children of Sephardic Jews moved too. One of these was Judah Touro, son of Rabbi Isaac Touro, who had been the first rabbi of Congregation Yeshuat Yisrael in Newport, Rhode Island. Judah Touro was one of the first Jews ever to settle in Louisiana. He was also one of the most successful. He earned his fortune as a merchant—taking goods from the North and selling them in the South for a commission—and by buying and selling real estate. When he arrived in New Orleans in 1802, it was a small Spanish-French village. By 1850, the year of his death, it was a great city, and he had done much to help it grow.

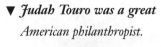

▼ *Judah Touro was a great American philanthropist.*

Peddling became the most important Jewish business in America. By 1850 about 10,000 Jewish peddlers were at work.

The Louisiana Purchase

President Thomas Jefferson purchased the Louisiana Territory from France in 1803. The land stretched from the Mississippi River to the Rocky Mountains, doubling the area of the United States.

Judah Touro built a hospital, a home for the poor, and the first public library in New Orleans. When he learned that there were no Jews left to support the synagogue in Newport, Rhode Island, he sent money to continue its upkeep. The building was renamed the Touro Synagogue in honor of his father.

At his death, Judah Touro left money to Jewish and non-Jewish institutions in seventeen cities throughout America. No American Jew had ever given so much to so many charitable agencies and causes.

Jews on the Frontier

When gold was discovered in California in 1848, many people rushed out West in search of fortune. Jews too joined this "gold rush" across the Rocky Mountains. As a result, two Yom Kippur services were held in San Francisco in 1849—one for Polish and English Jews and the other for German Jews. Each group went on to form its own synagogue.

▲ *In her memoirs, Amelia Ullmann of St. Paul wrote that winters in Minnesota were so cold she had to wrap herself in buffalo hides to keep warm.*

▲ *Horse-drawn stagecoaches provided transportation over the California frontier. The Pescadero and San Mateo Stage Company was owned by the Levy brothers.*

▼ *Prospectors panned for gold in the rivers.*

▶ *Levi Strauss became a millionaire selling the popular work pants shown in this advertisement. We've been wearing Levi's jeans ever since. Do you have any?*

Jewish Family Names

Michael Goldwater's original last name (surname) was Goldwasser. Many Jews changed or shortened their last names when they came to America. In some cases, immigration officials who could not spell a long, unusual-sounding Jewish name, such as Wallechinsky, shortened it (to Wallace). Some Jews, like Goldwasser, changed their own names to make them sound more American.

✧ *Find out if your surname was changed.*

✧ *What was the original name?*

✧ *How about your mother's family name?*

✧ *Have there been famous people who had the same last name as you?*

Levi Strauss, who followed the gold seekers, called the "forty-niners," west, sold a new kind of denim work pants (later nicknamed "Levis"). The company he founded became one of the most successful in America.

Other German Jews stopped in the Rockies to open stores during the 1859 rush for gold that had been found near Denver. When gold was discovered in Arizona in 1862, Jews set up shops in Phoenix and Tombstone. Michael and Joseph Goldwater opened the first of what became a chain of stores across the state. "Big Mike" Goldwater, a Jewish settler, was the grandfather of Arizona senator and one-time presidential candidate Barry Goldwater. One Jewish woman in Tombstone, Josephine Sarah Marcus, gained a place among the legends of the Wild West for living as the common-law wife of lawman and gunfighter Wyatt Earp for forty-seven years.

I n 1825 Mordecai Manuel Noah tried to establish a Jewish colony called Ararat near Buffalo, New York, but no settlers came. ***Why do you think Mordecai Manuel Noah chose the name Ararat for his colony?***

(Ararat is the name of the mountain on which Noah's ark landed after the biblical flood.)

The frontier was not always to the west. Some Jews went south. In Florida, Jews were among the founders of Miami, Key West, and Jacksonville. And long before the German Jews arrived, there were Sephardic Jews living in the state.

The first Jews in Texas had probably forgotten their Jewish heritage. They were the children and grandchildren of *conversos* who had come to Mexico in the sixteenth century. German Jews began arriving in Texas in the 1820s. Between the years 1850 and 1871 congregations were founded in Houston, Galveston, Brownsville, and Dallas.

Most of the Jews on the frontier were peddlers, merchants, and traders, but there were also physicians, lawyers, judges, government officials, and even a few plantation owners. Wherever they went, the pattern of Jewish settlement remained basically the same: They set up businesses and offices; they purchased land for a cemetery; they organized a congregation; then as they prospered and their numbers grew, they built a synagogue and school.

▲ *Louis Wolfson was a city commissioner in Key West, Florida. This is his store on Duval Street.*

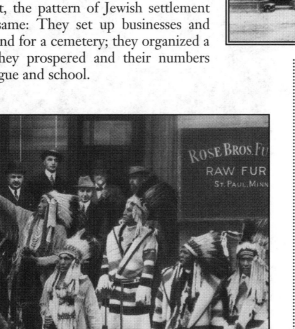

▲ *In 1911 the four Rose brothers posed with Blackfoot Indians in front of their fur company in St. Paul, Minnesota.*

Frontier Facts

By 1866 there were about 100 Jews living in Denver.

Jacksonville was the site of the first organized Jewish community in Florida.

It is estimated that 200 Jews fought for the independence of Texas.

Add another fact about Jewish life on the frontier that you learned in this chapter.

◄ *Uriah Phillips Levy*

The First Jewish Commodore

At the age of ten Uriah Phillips Levy went to sea as a cabin boy. When he was in his twenties, he became the captain of a sailing ship.

During the War of 1812 between Great Britain and the United States, Levy enlisted in the U.S. Navy. He was appointed a ship's master, but he was not a typical ship's master. He was constantly in trouble, partly because he had a sharp temper, but mainly because he was a Jew. He faced court-martial six times. But he always held that being a Jew was his right, protected by the Constitution.

It was common practice in those days to flog (whip) sailors. Levy was strongly opposed to such harsh punishment and allowed no sailor to be whipped on the ships he commanded. Because of his unpopular stand on this issue, Levy was demoted. He managed to have a special congressional court of inquiry look into the charges against him, and he was found innocent of any wrongdoing. He was later promoted to the high post of commodore.✪

Eventually Congress passed regulations outlawing the practice of flogging. This was Uriah Phillips Levy's proudest accomplishment. He always said he was the "father of the law for the abolition of the barbarous practice of corporal punishment in the Navy of the United States."

✪ A **commodore** is a naval officer ranking above a captain and below a rear admiral.

The Straus Family

Lazarus and Sara Straus and their sons arrived in America from Bavaria in the late 1840s. While Lazarus learned English, he struggled as a peddler—carrying pins and pots, diapers and tablecloths, bolts and nails from plantation to plantation in Georgia. Finally he saved enough money to open a small store in the town of Talbotton. During the Civil War money was scarce, and by the end of the war business was failing. Gathering up his courage, Straus moved his family to New York City, where he sold dishes and glassware.

In 1874 his three sons—Isidor, Nathan, and Oscar—rented the basement in the Macy store in New York and set up a crockery department. Soon the brothers became partners in R. H. Macy and Company, and by 1896 they were the sole owners of the business. Under their direction Macy's grew to become the largest department store in the world.

One of the Straus brothers, Isidor, devoted much of his personal time to the Educational Alliance of New York, a group formed to help new immigrants adjust to life in America. Another brother, Oscar, became the U.S. secretary of commerce and labor—the first Jew to ever serve in a U.S. presidential cabinet.

The peddler's life was not easy. The merchandise he carried on his back could weigh up to 150 pounds. The peddler endured thieves, bad weather, and sickness. Yet if he was persistent and hardworking, the peddler could rise to be an owner of a small general store. Some even founded famous department stores.

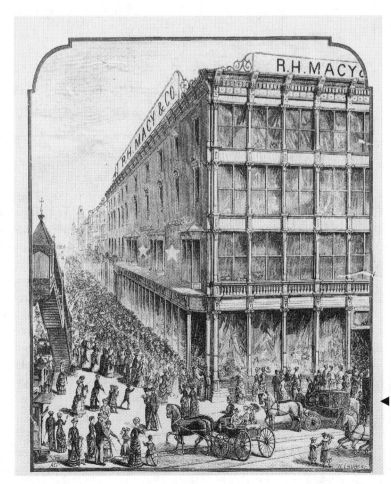

◄ *The Straus family developed Macy's into the biggest department store in the world.*

Nathan, the middle Straus brother, was known for his generosity. In hard winters during the 1890s he gave away more than a million buckets of coal to the unemployed. He built houses for the poor, where they could sleep and eat for a nickel a day.

Visiting Brussels, Straus saw Louis Pasteur demonstrate his new method of making milk safe. Pasteurizing milk partially sterilizes it, destroying harmful bacteria. On his return to the United States, Straus set up pasteurization plants, distributing free pasteurized milk to the poor. Thousands of babies were saved from illness and death by the safer milk. Within twenty years every state in the Union adopted laws requiring milk to be pasteurized.

Nathan Straus gave away nearly two-thirds of his fortune to help Jews in Eretz Yisrael. In gratitude, in 1928 the new city of Natanya was named after him.

Other German Jews

The success story was much the same for many other German Jews: Names like Gimbel, Altman, Seligman, Lazarus, and Guggenheim represented vast fortunes. They built mansions, sent their children to college, and took their families on European vacations.

But most of all they set aside parts of their fortunes to help the poor—Jews and non-Jews alike. Adolphus Solomons, a close friend of Abraham Lincoln, was a co-founder of the American Red Cross. Adolph Sutro donated his estate to the city of San Francisco. It became Sutro Heights Park, and anyone, rich or poor, could come there to spend an afternoon visiting the museum and aquarium that he gave to the city. Solomon Guggenheim donated an art museum to New York City and his children set up a free dental clinic for the city's children.

▲ *Adolph Sutro served as mayor of San Francisco from 1894 to 1896.*

What did Nathan Straus do to help the homeless in New York City in the 1890s? • How can we respond to this problem today?

◄ *Born to a wealthy German Jewish family in Cincinnati, Lillian Wald was educated at New York Hospital's School of Nursing. Her visiting nurses taught immigrant women how to care for their children.*

David Belasco introduced electrical lighting to the theatrical stage.

Others brought their skills and inventiveness to American life. Through his work as a director and playwright, David Belasco brought nearly 400 plays to the American stage. Emile Berliner improved Bell's telephone by inventing the transmitter that made sound clearer, and he invented the microphone that made radio and movies possible. He also built the first working helicopter, which he tested in flight himself. Lillian Wald started the nation's first Visiting Nurse's Service and urged the U.S. Congress to organize the federal Children's Bureau.

Looking Ahead

Of course not all German Jewish immigrants created department stores or achieved great wealth. Yet on the whole the German Jews became a comfortable group of middle-class merchants. Just as they were beginning to live the good life that America promised, their simple formula for the future was shattered. Everything was about to change. Events happening half a world away were soon to bring all Jews into a closer alliance.

▼ *Emile Berliner improved Thomas Edison's phonograph by inventing the flat record.*

1881 *Mass migration of Jews from Eastern Europe begins.*

1917 *Revolution installs a Communist government in Russia.*

1921 *U.S. immigration law ends Eastern Europea[n] mass migration.*

Also in this chapter: The year a Russian tsar was assassinated. *What was his name?*

The Eastern European Jews Arrive

In this pogrom ▶
*in Kiev, Jews were
beaten while the
police looked on.*

I t was 1881—a year of great turmoil in Russia—and the Jews were being blamed for everything that went wrong. When the weather was bad, the Jews were blamed. When a disease wiped out the crops, the Jews were blamed. Finally, when Tsar Alexander II was assassinated, the government blamed the Jews. Russian leaders helped to organize mobs of peasants to loot and burn Jewish homes and businesses. These organized riots were called pogroms,◉ and 1881 became known as "the Year of the Pogroms."

Legend says that in the 1880s a Russian government official announced a simple formula for dealing with the Jews: "Force one-third to emigrate, another third to convert to Christianity, and the remainder to die of starvation." In 1882 Russia issued "The May Laws," which forced Jews to leave the little villages and towns they had lived in for generations and move to cities. But in the cities there was no work for them, and often no housing. In 1903 another series of pogroms began, lasting to the end of 1906.

◉ The **pogroms** were organized massacres of helpless people.

◄ **This street scene is typical** *of the kind of small town, or* shtetl, *in which many Eastern European Jews lived. In one year, from 1905 to 1906, more than 650 Jewish villages in Russia were destroyed.*

The Jewish Response

Russia controlled the largest Jewish community in the world. The Jews were poor and they were persecuted. What could they do?

A few joined the new Zionist movement; they dreamed of creating a Jewish homeland. A handful left to become farmers in Eretz Yisrael. Some Jews in cities like Odessa and Kiev became socialists and communists, planning for a revolution that would make all Russians equal. Some Jews ignored the danger, refusing to leave their synagogues and great academies of Jewish learning.

A huge number of Polish and Russian, Galician, Hungarian, and Romanian Jews looked toward America. With each new pogrom more Jews left. They walked, rode in wagons, or if they had enough money, took the railroads to reach the sea so they could sail for America. They longed for the sight of New World harbors, such as Boston, Philadelphia, Baltimore, and Galveston. But for most the first sight of land was New York.

America——A Better Place to Go?

The Jewish immigrants crossed the Atlantic on steamships, often traveling in the cheapest steerage class. Some 15 percent of Eastern European Jewry—more than 2 million people—made the journey. They were not alone. Nearly 33 million other Europeans came during these same years of mass migration.⊙ The basic reason for this migration was the widespread poverty in Eastern Europe.

Between the years 1881 and 1924 more than 2.5 million Jews came to the United States from Eastern Europe.

⊙ **Migration** *is a movement of people (or animals) from one land or area to another.*

EMMA LAZARUS

Emma Lazarus gained fame as a poet. In 1883 she entered a poetry contest organized to raise money to build a pedestal for the Statue of Liberty. Her prize-winning poem, written in honor of the Russian Jews, was inscribed on the base of the statue. It says, in part:

Give me your tired, your poor,
Your huddled masses yearning to breathe free,
The wretched refuse of your teeming shore,
Send these, the homeless, tempest-tost to me,
I lift my lamp beside the golden door.

▼ *If weather permitted, passengers in steerage might be able to enjoy a few moments on the ship's deck.*

Not all who came were pleased with America. One of the most famous immigrants was the Yiddish writer Sholem Rabinowitz, better-known as Sholem Aleichem. He arrived in 1906 but returned to Europe after only a few months, finding American Jews raw and undignified compared with the great scholars of Europe. Later, when World War I broke out, he was forced to move his family back to New York. He died there in 1916, still complaining that America was an uncomfortable place for "real" Jews.

Most of the rabbis of Eastern Europe refused to go to America, and some told their followers that America was not a fit place for Jews to live. In 1893 one of the great European rabbis, Israel Meir Ha-Cohen, ruled against any further migration to America. He told his followers that it was better to suffer persecution in Russia than to move to a land "which causes turning away from God." Nevertheless, Jews continued to leave for America by the thousands.

As they left the boat, immigrants often cried out in Yiddish, "Leben zol Columbus!" ***Can you guess what it means?***
(Long live Columbus!)

The Arrival

Coming off the ship in New York harbor, the immigrants entered the halls of Ellis Island. American immigration officials asked them their names, where they were from, and where they were going. Immigrants had to pass a physical examination before entering the United States. If doctors found the trachoma virus, for example, an eye disease that was quite common in Eastern Europe, the immigrant was sent back to Europe.

Those who were admitted were taken on a short ferry ride to Battery Park. There people were waiting. Some immigrants were greeted by relatives. Others were met by agents from boarding houses, offering places to stay. There were employers offering jobs for tinsmiths who were willing to go to Kentucky or cobblers who were willing to live in Albany. Still other employers were looking for people to work in the New York City garment industry.

My Immigrant Ancestors

The vast majority of today's American Jews are descendants of immigrants who arrived between 1881 and 1924. The individuals in your family who made the difficult decision to leave their homes and travel to America had a great impact on your life. Find out about your immigrant ancestors.

✧ From which country did your father's family and your mother's family come originally?

✧ When did your ancestors (on both sides) come to America?

✧ Where did they land when they arrived in this country?

▲ *You can visit this building on Ellis Island which has been made into a museum.*

This photograph shows ▶
a typical business day on
the Lower East Side in
1912. The noisy street was
jammed with carts full of
merchandise for sale.

Immigrant Life

New York's overcrowded Lower East Side was the first home for many of the newly arrived Eastern European Jews.

Back in Europe most of them had lived in small villages hardly changed since the seventeenth century. In America things seemed to be changing all the time. Back in Europe most of them had been shopkeepers, tinsmiths, cobblers, jewelers, tailors, and millers. In America they had to train for new jobs in factories and sweatshops.

The immigrants brought few ▲ *possessions with them — a few pieces of clothing, a prayer book, a picture of the family left behind. This immigrant was photographed in 1890 as he prepared for Shabbat in his basement room.*

◀ *Some immigrants were too old to learn a new trade and too poor to set up a shop. They supported themselves by buying and selling old clothes from pushcarts.*

▲ *Volunteers from the National Council of Jewish Women met newly arrived women from Russia. The council opened a home for unmarried women and another for Jewish girls from troubled families.*

Helping the New Immigrants

The new immigrants needed help in finding a job and a place to live. They had to learn English. Some of the German Jews wanted to help the new immigrants simply because aiding the poor was a Jewish tradition—a *mitzvah*. Others tried to help because the impoverished Russians were an embarrassment to them. For whatever reason they reached out a helping hand.

With donated funds the Young Men's Hebrew Association (YMHA) opened on the Lower East Side, offering classes in English and teaching the values of democracy. Classes for new immigrants were also organized in Baltimore, by Henrietta Szold. The importance of this kind of instruction was soon realized, and classes for immigrants (night-schools) sprang up throughout the country.

Russian Jews continued to arrive daily. Sometimes as many as 5,000 arrived in a single month! There just wasn't room enough on the Lower East Side of New York. The Hebrew Emigrants Aid Society helped these newcomers resettle in Pennsylvania, Wisconsin, Colorado, and all points west.

During the 1970s a new wave of Russian immigrants reached America. **Find out how American Jews helped those new settlers.**

Graduates of a night-school ▶ *citizenship class proudly display American flags.*

Pathways to Fame and Fortune

The streets of America's cities were not paved with gold, as the immigrants had thought. Instead, the streets taught the immigrants many lessons, and not always good ones. Some of the immigrants turned to crime. Sometimes immigrant children would steal from pushcarts, pick pockets, or join street gangs. Most of them grew up to become honest and productive members of society, but a few continued their criminal activities as adults.

A better way to riches was through sports. For many years the Lower East Side produced one great boxer after another, such as Benny Leonard, Ruby Goldstein, and Barney Ross. In one year in the 1920s Jews held seven of the nine boxing championships.

A third path to riches was entertainment. In Europe there had been Jewish klezmer bands, stand-up comics, and many small theater groups. In America the Jews discovered the vaudeville theater. The history of live theater in the United States includes the names of many Jewish entertainers, writers, producers, and musicians. Among them are Irving Berlin, George Gershwin, Lee Shubert, Fanny Brice, Zero Mostel, and Jerome Kern.

All of these pathways to fame and fortune were well worn with Jewish steps. And all of them led to the explosion of Jewish culture that would take place in the second half of the twentieth century.

▲ **Benny Leonard held the** *world lightweight boxing title from 1917 to 1925.*

Which famous Yiddish actor starred at the Grand Theater in 1900? • In what play? (Jacob P. Adler in The Broken Hearts)

*◄ Fanny Brice appeared
in Manhattan vaudeville
shows as a singer and
dancer. She starred in the
famous Zeigfeld Follies
from 1910 to 1923. Her
life story was told in the
Broadway production and
film of* Funny Girl. *Both
starred another famous
Jewish entertainer,
Barbra Streisand.*

Looking Ahead

While the German Jews of America could do nothing to stop the pogroms in Russia, they knew that they had to help the Eastern European Jews who poured into America by the thousands. And they did.

Who could imagine the changes that the Russian and Polish Jews would make in the American Jewish community and, in fact, in America itself? That is another chapter.

George Gershwin composed for the Broadway ►
stage and symphony orchestras. His Rhapsody in
Blue *and* Porgy and Bess *have become American
classics. Irving Berlin (right) wrote more than
1,000 popular songs. One of his most famous hits is
"God Bless America." He also wrote Broadway
shows such as* Call Me Madam *and*
Annie Get Your Gun.

6 Organizing Jewish Life

The German Jews wanted to "Americanize" their Eastern European cousins. The Russian Jews wanted to do things their own way.

When it came to religion, things were most confusing. Back in Russia there was one chief rabbi and a board to govern all of the synagogues. In America there were still very few rabbis. In 1887 fifteen of the largest Orthodox synagogues in America invited Rabbi Jacob Josephs, the rabbi of Vilna, Lithuania, to become their chief rabbi. But after the rabbi arrived, the congregation could not agree on how to pay his salary. Some wanted to raise money for the rabbi by putting a tax on all kosher foods, but others protested that kosher food already cost too much. Nothing was settled, and the idea of uniting under one chief rabbi was abandoned. In 1902 another attempt was made to unite the Orthodox community when the Union of Orthodox Rabbis was created. Even this did not succeed. Other "unions" of rabbis followed, such as the Rabbinical Council of America, which was made up entirely of Orthodox rabbis who were ordained in America.

▲ *This charcoal drawing, sketched in 1902 by Jacob Epstein, is titled "Going to the Synagogue."*

Small synagogues ▶ sprang up all over New York City. Immigrants who had come from the same towns in Eastern Europe often prayed together. If they could not afford to build a synagogue, they met in rented tenement rooms or stores.

◄ *When Solomon Schechter heard about a* genizah✿ *in Egypt, he went there and found more than 100,000 manuscript leaves and fragments stored in a Cairo synagogue. They were sent to England, where Schechter began the massive work of piecing them together. We can imagine him taking a break from his work of translating to read the letter of invitation to come to New York that would change his life.*

▼ *The three buildings constructed at the corner of Manhattan's Broadway and 122nd Street remain the heart of the JTS campus.*

Conservative Judaism and Solomon Schechter

Seeing that the Eastern European Jews could not organize themselves, the Reform German Jews decided to lend a hand. Back in 1886 a school called the Jewish Theological Seminary (JTS) had been established to train "traditional" American rabbis. Ten years later, it was deep in debt. A famous scholar, Cyrus Adler, believed that JTS could train some of the Eastern European immigrants to become Conservative rabbis who could then help to "Americanize" the Orthodox Russian Jews. Adler's idea appealed to some leaders among the German Reform Jews and they gave him $500,000, a huge sum of money in those days. Together they invited the scholar Solomon Schechter to head the reborn Jewish Theological Seminary. Less than a year later, in 1902, Schechter arrived in New York.

Some of the graduates of his seminary were hired by the more traditional German synagogues, but the majority of the rabbis who graduated from JTS led traditional synagogues for Russian Jewish immigrants. By 1913 Schechter had organized sixteen congregations into the United Synagogue of America. He had officially founded the Conservative movement. Like Isaac Mayer Wise before him, Schechter had forged another major movement for American Jews.

✿ A **genizah** is a special storage space for hiding worn-out Hebrew books and manuscripts that often contain God's name and therefore should not be destroyed.

A Fight for Jewish Rights

Life on New York's Lower East Side seemed strange and disorganized. The streets were teeming with people jostling one another. Pushcarts were filled with "bargains," and people, still dressed in clothing brought from the Old Country, pushed to get close to them. Reporting on conditions on the Lower East Side, American newspapers and magazines began to say that all Jews were "rowdy" and "strange looking." Some of America's better hotels and resorts put out large signs saying "No Jews Allowed," and some of the finer restaurants refused to serve Jews altogether.

MENAUHANT HOTEL

$$$$$$$$$$$$$$ MENAUHANT, MASS. $$$$$$$$$$$$$$

THIS House, is situated in Falmouth Township, on the South Shore of Cape Cod, at the confluence of Nantucket and Vineyard Sounds, it is directly on the beach, and is nearly surrounded by water; it is owned and managed by Mr. Floyd Travis, and will be open for the season of 1906, on June 16th.

MENAUHANT WHARF.

A great many conditions combine to make Menauhant the most delightful summer resort on Cape Cod.

We have no HEBREW patronage.

*I*f you were denied the right to do something because you were Jewish, how would you respond?

▲ *This advertisement appeared in 1906. Where was the hotel located? Would you have been a welcome guest?*

The Great Hoax

The idea was old, but beginning in Russia in the 1890s it was used in a new way. A newspaper printed a report of secret meetings supposedly held by Jewish leaders in Switzerland plotting to seize world power by overthrowing all governments. Of course, there had never been any such meetings, but people often believe what they see in print. In 1905 the Russian army published the newspaper articles as a book called *Protocols of the Elders of Zion*. After World War I copies were reprinted in the London newspaper the *Morning Post* and in Detroit, Michigan, in the *Dearborn Independent*, a newspaper owned by the famous automobile manufacturer Henry Ford.

Leaders of the American Jewish Committee went into action against Ford and against the *Protocols*. They wrote letter after letter to Henry Ford, also publishing many of them in newspapers. At first Ford insisted that the *Protocols* were real. But in 1927 he issued an apology to Louis Marshall, president of the American Jewish Committee. Ford admitted that the book was a lie from start to finish. Despite this, from time to time some anti-Jewish groups still reprint the *Protocols of the Elders of Zion*.

◄ *Louis Marshall was one of America's leading lawyers. He fought case after case in the search for civil rights. One of his lifelong battles was fought against the Ku Klux Klan, which once numbered 4 million members.*

B'nai B'rith

Outside of the religious movements the first major Jewish organization founded was B'nai B'rith. In 1843 a large number of New York Jews united to form this group based on the ethical teachings of Judaism. Today there are more than 500,000 members in B'nai B'rith, which sets up Hillel Houses and Jewish activities on college campuses and supports the Anti-Defamation League.

The Jews felt that Americans would change their opinions if they understood more about Judaism and knew what Jews had done for America. They created an organization called the American Jewish Committee. It was made up of German Jews who were active in civic affairs, people such as Adolph Ochs (publisher of *The New York Times*), Louis Marshall (a famous lawyer), and Jacob Schiff (an important financier). On November 11, 1906, they met with fifty others and created the American Jewish Committee "to protect Jewish rights wherever they are threatened." They set out to educate the American public about Jews, about Judaism, and about the meaning of America's laws of equality.

An Attempt at Self-Government

In 1908 in New York an attempt was made to establish a Jewish communal self-government. This movement, called the Kehillah,✡ tried to bring together the various Jewish groups into a single organization. In Europe it was possible for one Jewish organization to speak for all the Jews in a community. But America was a free country; people had the right to choose. There was no law that said the Jews had to join a special group, and American Jews had diverse loyalties—to their jobs, to their families, and to other groups in American life. The Kehillah managed to attract only 15 percent of the organizations in the New York Jewish community. Perhaps the greatest success was the establishment of the Board of Jewish Education of New York, which continues to this day.

✡ *Kehillah* is a Hebrew word meaning "community."

World War I

In 1914 the world went to war. Most Americans waited and watched, hoping America would be able to stay out of the Great War in Europe. But not the new immigrants from Russia. Their relatives back home were suffering. The suffering grew even worse during and after the Russian Revolution in 1917. Jewish shops and homes were looted and burned, Jewish women were raped, and Jewish men and women were murdered.

The tragedy in Russia brought Jews together in a new way. In 1914 American Jews of all kinds organized to form the Joint Distribution Committee of the American Funds for the Needs of Jewish War Sufferers, nicknamed the Joint. During World War I the Joint raised almost $17 million. The money was sent to aid Jews in Russia, Poland, and the Baltic states. Houses were rebuilt, shops were restored, and families were given money to buy food and clothing. America's Jews now found they were a chief means of support for Jews throughout the world. Just before peace was declared, another new organization, the American Jewish Congress, was formed to send a delegation to the peace talks in Versailles. The American Jewish Congress was concerned with the many problems facing Jews in Europe, and its delegation ensured that the treaties that ended the war included a guarantee for the rights of all minorities in Europe—Jewish and non-Jewish.

Y ou have read about two Jewish organizations known by the initials AJC. *Can you name them?*

(American Jewish Committee and American Jewish Congress)

ORT

Another American Jewish organization for aid was set up in 1923. ORT is the Organization for Rehabilitation through Training. ORT provides vocational schools for Jews around the world, teaching boys and girls the new skills needed for jobs in the industrial world.

◄ *In this photograph taken in 1919, rabbis supervise the first shipment of kosher meat sent to starving Jewish communities in Poland.*

Is your Jewish community federated?

Find out how much money your Jewish community raised last year. Which local agencies are supported by this fund-raising effort? How much of the money was sent to Israel?

F rom 1946 through 1962 American Jews raised $2.3 billion in Federation/UJA fund-raising drives. *How is your math? • Figure out the average amount of money raised in each of those seventeen years.* (An average of $135.3 million each year.)

Organizing Jewish Charities

During the 1920s, as new congregations were built in middle-class neighborhoods, America's Jews experimented with a new way to raise money for the many needs at home and around the world. Organizations like B'nai B'rith and Hadassah were joined by new charitable associations called federations.

Federations raised funds in one community-wide effort called a campaign. The funds raised were then divided among the many charities that required them. In this way individual charities received larger sums than if they had competed against one another.

Almost all of the larger Jewish communities were federated. The first Federation of Jewish Philanthropies was established in Boston in 1895. The agencies it supported included an orphanage, a relief fund, an employment bureau, and a burial society. Cincinnati organized its federation a year later. Baltimore federated in 1907, San Francisco did so in 1910, and New York established its Federation of Jewish Philanthropies in 1917.

By the 1950s communities as small as 3,000 or 4,000 Jews had organized their own federations. To help one another, the federations created a national organization called the Council of Jewish Federations and Welfare Funds. The CJF studied national Jewish causes to determine which were the most deserving. In this way the American Jewish community supported old-age homes, Jewish community centers, free loan societies, family services, Jewish education bureaus, and Jewish hospitals. Funds raised locally were also shared with the United Jewish Appeal, which was devoted to helping Jewish causes overseas, particularly in the State of Israel.

◀ *These young people in Tucson, Arizona, are running in a race to raise money to help Russian Jews.*

TZEDAKAH

Most people think of the Hebrew word *tzedakah* as charity, but the word actually means "righteousness." When Jews give charity, we do so not only because it is a good and kind thing to do but because it is the right thing to do.

Maimonides, a famous Jewish philosopher, classified people who perform acts of *tzedakah* into eight groups. The eighth level, according to Maimonides, is the highest. Do you agree?

1. One who is asked and gives unwillingly.

2. One who gives less than is appropriate but gives cheerfully.

3. One who gives a proper amount after being asked.

4. One who gives before being asked.

5. One who gives and does not know the receiver.

6. One who gives and does know the receiver but remains anonymous.

7. Both giver and receiver are unknown to each other.

8. One who helps people provide for themselves so they will not need future help.

What can you do as a volunteer at a home for the aged?

How would Maimonides have rated these acts of tzedakah?

- You plant a tree in Israel in honor of your mother's birthday.
- You tutor a Russian immigrant so that he can do better in school.
- You donate the clothing you have outgrown to charity.
- You help an elderly neighbor rake leaves from her yard.
- You ride your bicycle in a bikathon to raise money for UJA.
- You bring cans of food to a Thanksgiving food drive.

◄ Kaplan's idea that Jews should create a "Jewish civilization" by living as a community influenced the Jewish Community Center (JCC) movement. In a JCC, Jews can participate in sports, arts, and study. Do you belong to a JCC?

A New Religious Movement

Beginning in 1909 Rabbi Mordecai M. Kaplan served as head of the Teachers Institute of the Jewish Theological Seminary. Through the years his students became loyal followers of his ideas. He taught that Judaism is an ever-growing "religious civilization." Like all civilizations, Judaism has a land, a language, and a culture. Like a religion, Judaism encourages its adherents to wrestle with the idea of God and keep rituals in their homes and synagogues. A synagogue, Kaplan said, should be a "community center."

Kaplan believed in giving women full equality in Judaism. In 1922 his daughter Judith was the first Jewish woman in America to become a Bat Mitzvah.

At first Kaplan was satisfied just teaching his students, but in 1935 he began publishing the *Reconstructionist Magazine* to share his ideas with other American Jews. His many followers soon convinced him that his Reconstructionism was really distinct from Conservative Judaism. In 1940 Kaplan founded the Reconstructionist Foundation, and in 1968 the Reconstructionist Rabbinical College was established in Philadelphia to train rabbis. Mordecai M. Kaplan had given birth to a new Jewish movement.

Looking Ahead

Organizations like the federations, B'nai B'rith, the American Jewish Committee, the Joint, ORT, and the American Jewish Congress became as central to Jewish life in America as the synagogues. And like the synagogues, they continue their important work today.

Yet the work of organizing was just beginning. The next organizations the Jews built would change not only Jewish life but the life of all Americans.

| 1901 | President McKinley is fatally shot. | 1911 | Triangle Shirtwaist fire. | 1928 | Disney releases first Mickey Mouse film. |

Also in this chapter: The year the Free Synagogue was established. *What was the founding rabbi's name?*

7 The Labor Movement

◀ *There were few decent jobs for new immigrants. Many people were forced to work in sweatshops, where they sat at their sewing machines for twelve to eighteen hours a day. If workers complained, they were fired—there were always new immigrants to take their place.*

By the early 1900s America was settling down. There was little need for peddlers anymore; there were stores in cities and small towns nearly everywhere. Yet there was a great need for workers in big cities, especially in New York. A new clothing industry made ready-to-wear garments—dresses, men's suits, blouses, and shirts—that were sold throughout the United States. There were clothing factories through-out America, but New York City was the center of this growing garment trade.

Most of the garment workers were new immigrants who could not speak English. They sat hunched over sewing machines, putting together pieces of fabric that had been cut in a factory. Their sewing machines were usually in rented rooms or basements that were so poorly ventilated that they were called sweatshops. Sweatshop pay was very low, and work hours were very long. In summer the sweatshops were too hot; in winter they were too cold. The light was always too dim. Work areas were hardly ever cleaned. Many workers suffered from tuberculosis and other lung diseases.

▲ *A Yiddish newspaper,* the Jewish Daily Forward, *became a powerful voice of the labor movement.*

▲ *The seal of the American Federation of Labor shows hands clasped in solidarity.*

Samuel Gompers, Champion of Labor

Samuel Gompers was born in England and came to New York at the age of thirteen. Back in London he had been a student in the Jewish Free School, but at age ten he was forced to leave and begin work. Like many other Jews, he would work all day, then go to school at night. "At night school," he said, "I was taught Hebrew . . . that honorable language that unlocked a literature of wonderful beauty and wisdom." Gompers never forgot his lessons in Judaism. When he spoke, his words were filled with Jewish ideas. When he saw the poverty and misery and suffering in the sweatshops, he thought of how the Bible hated slavery. He wanted to see changes made.

By age fifteen Gompers was working in a cigar factory in New York. In 1872 he joined the Cigar Makers' Union and soon became president of his local chapter. His fight for the rights of cigar makers was so successful that he was soon made vice-president of the national union.

By 1886 Samuel Gompers was president of what would soon be the American Federation of Labor, the fastest-growing union of workers in the United States. His first major fight was to win an eight-hour workday. He also fought against child labor, and he organized health centers and schools for workers.

Through all his work Gompers never lost sight of his Jewish heritage. "I failed to see," he wrote, "how [people] whether Christian or Jewish could profit through the misery of human beings." When he died in 1924, the American Federation of Labor had grown to a membership of 5 million workers.

Samuel Gompers speaks ▶ at a meeting of 3,000 workers in 1909.

C*an You Imagine?* By the age of nine or ten, many immigrant children were working in sweatshops. By the age of fourteen young women were sitting at their work tables for as long as ten hours a day. *Do you think the labor movement helped you? • How?*

Other Unions and Strikes

Most labor unions were organized around a single trade. There was a union for cigar makers, another for garment workers, and so on. But at the beginning of the labor movement, in 1888, the leaders of the Russian Jewish immigrants organized a labor union called the United Hebrew Trades, which tried to organize all working Jews. The United Hebrew Trades was led by eighteen-year-old Morris Hillquit. He organized his first strike against the knee-pants makers of New York. Knee pants were almost as popular then as jeans are today, and most of the people who made them were women. The owners of the sweatshops were paying workers only seven dollars a week—no matter how hard they worked—and the workers had to purchase their own sewing machines and provide their own needles and thread.

One week after the strike began, the sweatshop bosses were offering raises and better working conditions and asking their workers to come back. Hillquit's strike was a success.

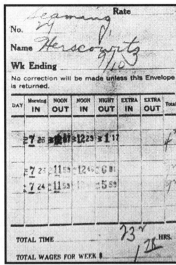

▲ *This garment worker pay envelope is from the early 1900s. How much money did the worker receive for 23 1/2 hours of work? How much did the worker earn per hour?*

A TEENAGE ACTIVIST

C lara Lemlich is shown in the middle of this painting with her hand raised. On November 22, 1909, when the workers of the ladies' shirtwaist (blouse) industry met to discuss whether or not to go on strike, she asked to speak: "I am a working girl. . . . What we are here for is to decide whether or not to strike. I offer a resolution that a general strike be declared—now!" There was wild cheering as thousands of workers raised their hands in agreement. This strike came to be known as the Uprising of the Twenty Thousand.

Women on the march ▶
during the 1909 shirt-
waist makers' strike.

Children at Work Today

The organization Childright Worldwide estimates that 100 million to 200 million children throughout the world did not go to school today because they were forced to work and that this number will reach 400 million by the year 2000.

Children in Pakistan weave carpets from 6:00 A.M. to 7:00 P.M. for less than twenty cents a day. If any of these children cry, they are beaten or chained to the loom. Children in India are often branded like cattle by their employers.

✦ *Do we have a responsibility to try to improve the conditions for workers abroad?*

✦ *What can we do to help?*

The Uprising of the Twenty Thousand

The International Ladies' Garment Workers' Union (ILGWU) led a major strike in 1909 that resulted in a history-making labor settlement. Twenty thousand women left their sewing tables to walk the picket lines. The strike was so successful that in 1910, 60,000 workers of the Cloakmakers' Union also went out on strike. This time it took the work of a Boston Jewish lawyer, Louis D. Brandeis (later a Supreme Court justice) to settle the strike. There were Jews on both sides, among the workers and among the owners. What impressed Brandeis most was that the two sides were actually willing to listen to one another. The settlement provided a model for future strike negotiations.

Three Labor Leaders

In Chicago, Sidney Hillman organized a strike of garment workers in 1910. Forty thousand workers followed him out of their shops, and managers were forced to listen to demands for higher pay and better working conditions. Hillman continued to serve the labor unions his whole life. He became a close friend and advisor of President Franklin D. Roosevelt.

In 1932 David Dubinsky took over the ILGWU and made it one of the most powerful unions in America. Dubinsky always spoke of himself as a "Jewish worker" and actively helped Jewish refugees from Europe and the small growing Jewish community in Eretz Yisrael.

Abraham Cahan helped found the *Jewish Daily Forward* and served as its editor from 1902 until his death in 1951. This Yiddish-language newspaper became a powerful voice of the labor movement. One of its most popular features was a column called "Bintel Brief" ("Bundle of Letters"), which answered readers' personal problems.

◀ *Newsboys pose in front of the* Forward *building on Manhattan's Lower East Side in 1909.*

From the "Bintel Brief," 1908

Esteemed Editor,

We were in the shop working when the boss came over to one of us and shouted, "You ruined the work. You'll have to pay for it!" Then the boss spat and walked away. Overcome with shame, the worker obviously felt that he had done wrong in not standing up for his honor and we could see the tears running down his cheeks. Did this man act correctly in remaining silent? Is the fact that he has a wife and five children reason enough for his refusal to defend himself?

ANSWER: The worker cannot help himself alone, but he must not remain alone and he must not remain silent. He must unite with his fellow workers and fight.

On March 25, 1911, a fire broke out in the top-story sweatshop of the Triangle Shirtwaist Company at the corner of Washington Place and Greene Street in New York. The women workers tried to escape, but they found the only fire exit blocked and sealed. The flames spread rapidly, feeding on the yards and yards of fabric in the loft. Many women were trapped by the flames, others died from the smoke that poured through the rooms, and some jumped out of the windows to their death on the street below.

When the fire was over, some 150 workers lay dead. Most of them were young Jewish women between the ages of sixteen and twenty-five. The workers of America went into mourning; so did the Jews of America. After that more Jews joined the labor union movement, and they demanded not just higher wages but, above all, safer workplaces for American workers.

During the Triangle fire there was little the firemen could do to save workers trapped in the building. Their ladders didn't reach the floors on fire, and neither did the water from their hoses. The workers who jumped fell with such great force that their bodies plunged through the firemen's nets.

A Rabbi for All Seasons

Among the great friends of the labor leaders was the outspoken Reform rabbi Stephen S. Wise of New York. In 1907 Stephen Wise founded the Free Synagogue and made two guarantees: complete freedom of speech for the rabbi and free membership to any Jew who wished to join but could not afford to pay dues. As the membership of the Free Synagogue grew, Rabbi Wise rented Carnegie Hall every Sunday for a special service. Newspapers sent reporters to listen to what this dynamic rabbi had to say about the issues of the day.

Wise spoke out on every front. He demanded better labor laws and called for laws against child labor, he opposed the continuing oppression of black Americans, and he championed the cause of the American Indian. But he wasn't just a great speaker. Whenever possible, he put his ideas into practice. In 1910 he became a founding member of the National Association for the Advancement of Colored People (NAACP) and in 1920 of the American Civil Liberties Union (ACLU). He was a founder of the American Jewish Congress and the Zionist Organization of America, which favored the establishment of a Jewish nation in the Holy Land. He hired a full-time social worker for his Free Synagogue to organize projects that reached out into the surrounding neighborhoods, the city, and the nation.

The Jewish Institute of Religion was a graduate school organized by Rabbi Stephen S. Wise to train rabbis and educators who would carry on his fight for social reforms.

At a time when religion and the labor movement seemed to be going in two different directions, Wise showed that they had common roots and common goals. Working together, religion and labor could be stronger and more effective in ensuring the freedom and well-being of the vast working class in America.

Rabbi Wise's Sunday morning ▶
sermons became the talk of the
town, drawing large numbers of
Jews and Christians alike.

Religion and Labor

The battles of the labor movement were fought and won in the streets and in the newspapers, not in the synagogues. However, rabbis and other religious leaders did not close their eyes to what was happening. In 1918 the Central Conference of American Rabbis declared that all Reform Jews should join the struggle for an eight-hour day, for a day of rest each week, and for a fair minimum wage for all workers. This was a remarkable decision. Many members of Reform congregations at that time were the owners and managers of the very sweatshops and factories against whom the rabbis spoke.

The National Labor Relations Act, passed by Congress in 1935, finally gave workers the right to organize and required employers to bargain with labor unions.

In 1933 the Conservative movement officially joined the Reform movement in its support of labor. But long before that time many Conservative rabbis had spoken out in favor of the labor movement. The same was true for many Orthodox rabbis, who called for better conditions, a shorter work week, and higher wages for the workers.

Social justice has always been an important value in Judaism. As one of its highest ideals the Jewish religion has always taught the pursuit of justice, and that idea was at the heart of the labor union movement.

Looking Ahead

All things change in time. Today you may hear people say that the labor unions have grown too powerful. Yet looking back on the history of labor in America, we can see how important the unions have been. They abolished child labor and guaranteed the basic rights of American workers.

Within the Jewish community the labor movement was a sign that the Jews of America were learning the skills of leadership that they would need in the years to come. The American Jewish community would soon find itself the foremost Jewish community in the world.

▲ *Joseph Schaffner was a senior partner of Hart Schaffner & Marx, the largest manufacturer of men's clothing in the world. Schaffner was unaware of conditions in his Chicago factories, so the 1910 garment workers' strike came as a surprise to him, and the criticism of the rabbis troubled him. Schaffner personally entered into negotiations with the strike committee, and because of his persistence and good will the strike was fairly settled.*

| 1907 | Nobel Prize for Physics is won by an American for the first time. | 1929 | The stock market crashes. | 1939 | Germany invades Poland. |

Also in this chapter: The year a famous Jewish lawyer was appointed to the U.S. Supreme Court. *What was his name?*

Coming of Age

In the early days of immigration both Jewish and non-Jewish newcomers had tried to change themselves in ways that would make them more "American." In the twentieth century, however, newcomers were arriving with a different idea. Using the traditions and cultures they brought from their homelands, they were changing what it meant *to be* American. Each new wave of immigrants—German, Irish, Italian, Jewish, Chinese, Japanese, Puerto Rican—brought new richness to the soil of the United States. Using their talents, they helped America grow into a mighty nation. America's Jews became a major force for American progress.

◄ *In 1907 the first Nobel Prize*✪ *for Physics won by an American was awarded to the Jewish scientist Albert Abraham Michelson.*

✪ The **Nobel Prize** is an international award for achievements in the sciences, literature, and other fields.

Albert Abraham Michelson

A Jewish immigrant from Prussia, Michelson became the most famous scientist of his day. His talent lay in the new science of physics. After many years of research he made a fantastic discovery: Using physics and mathematics together, Michelson was able to calculate the speed of light. This accomplishment made him world famous, but he was not through yet. Next he invented the interferometer, a device used to measure the diameter of faraway stars and to make close-up studies of radioactivity, vitamins, and human hormones.

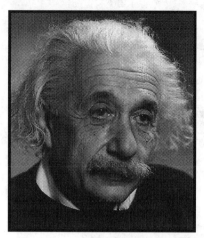

▲ *Albert Einstein*

Jewish Contributions to Science and Medicine

Joseph Goldberger was a scientist who pioneered preventive medicine. He studied a disease called pellagra. At the time it was thought that pellagra was caused by a germ, but Goldberger proved that the disease resulted from a diet lacking in niacin and protein. His finding laid the basis for the modern science of nutrition.

In 1921 the Nobel Prize for Physics was awarded to the famous Jewish scientist Albert Einstein. Einstein came to America in 1933 and continued his studies here. He was a supporter of Zionism and helped raise funds for the new Hebrew University in Jerusalem. His theory of relativity is considered the greatest single scientific discovery of modern times.

In science, medicine, and many other fields American Jews, living in freedom under the protection of the Constitution, were making major contributions to America and the world at large.

Another Jewish scientist, Selman A. Waksman, worked with a team of research scientists to isolate streptomycin, an antibiotic effective against many diseases, especially tuberculosis. For this discovery Waksman received the Nobel Prize in Physiology or Medicine in 1952.

Polio was a widespread children's disease that leaves its victims crippled and sometimes even kills them. In 1954 Jonas Salk developed the anti-polio vaccine that keeps us safe from this dreaded disease today.

▲ *Dr. Jonas Salk*

▲ *Dr. Selman A. Waksman*

The Changing Immigration Laws

Despite the contributions that immigrants were making to America, the doors of the United States were closing. The government decided to place limits on the number of immigrants who could enter the country. In 1924 Congress passed a law that allowed only 8,600 immigrants from Poland, Russia, and Romania to enter the United States in any one year.

The people of the United States were generally pleased by this law. There were many reasons. Those who had jobs were afraid of losing them to new immigrants who would work more cheaply. Some felt that mass immigration brought criminals to America. Others thought America could not prosper with so many new mouths to feed each year. There was also prejudice and fear.

After the Revolution of 1917 the Communists took over Russia. In the United States many government officials believed that there was a Jewish-Communist plan to take over the whole world. Some Jews— especially those who were part of the labor movement—had joined the American Communist Party. Later, when they realized that the Communists in Russia were anti-Semitic, most of them left the party. But the damage had been done. By the 1920s many Americans were convinced that most Jews were Communists and wanted to limit immigration to keep additional Jewish Communists out.

Jews already living in the United States were afraid to speak out against these new immigration laws. What would happen if the Congress were to turn the same policy toward Jews already living in America? Two church groups did speak out. The National Catholic Welfare Conference and the Federal Council of Protestant Churches asked that limits on immigration not be based on country of origin. But these voices of reason were not popular, and the law remained. The years of welcoming Jewish immigrants to the United States were over.

Expert Testimony

In 1924 "experts" testifying before Congress claimed that Jews and other Eastern Europeans were "biologically inferior." They used the results of English-language intelligence tests that had been given to new immigrants entering the U.S. Army to prove that those from England were the most intelligent while Russians, Italians, and Poles were stupid.

No one seemed to notice the most obvious reason for the results of these tests. *Do you?*

The Rosenwald family story shows the many directions in which America's Jewish community was working in the period before World War II.

In 1895 a young German Jew named Julius Rosenwald had bought an interest in a mail order company founded by a man named Sears. Rosenwald used his talents to help create a great chain of retail stores—Sears, Roebuck & Company. The Rosenwalds used their fortune to support the Tuskegee Institute, a school for blacks in Alabama. They established the Rosenwald Fund, which by 1932 had set up more than 5,000 black elementary schools in the rural South. They also established the Museum of Science and Industry in Chicago and sent aid to European Jews.

The Rosenwald children also became known for their generosity. One son became a leader in the Jewish federation movement. One daughter became a devoted Zionist, using her great fortune to help Jews buy land and build new towns and cities in the Holy Land. Yet another daughter became a community leader in the South, fighting for equal voting rights and fair politics in Louisiana.

The collapse of Wall Street's New York Stock Market in 1929 triggered the Great Depression.

Jewish Life

Jews in the major cities continued to work mainly in business and the trades.

More and more businesses were becoming corporations, and the new corporations were run by boards of directors, not individuals. As prejudice spread throughout the country, few Jews were ever promoted to the top levels of these large companies. There was also discrimination against Jews in hiring—non-Jews were often hired for a position even when a Jewish applicant was better qualified. In many cities the Jews also found that there were certain neighborhoods where no Jew could buy a home.

Just as the Jews were thinking that a major battle of equal rights would have to begin, the entire business community of the United States was shaken to its very roots.

◀ *Local agencies tried to provide help for the hungry. In some stores people could exchange relief tickets for food.*

▼ *The university bears the name of Louis D. Brandeis, who was appointed a justice of the U.S. Supreme Court in 1916—the first Jew to hold this position.*

The Great Depression

The Depression of 1929 struck with the explosive force of a tornado. In one day thousands of people lost entire life savings. Tens of thousands lost jobs. Farmers lost their farms. Stores lost their customers, and many businesses closed their doors forever. People took any odd jobs they could find just to keep feeding their families. Doctors and lawyers accepted chickens and eggs as payment for their services. Some people tried to earn a living by selling apples on the city streets. Nearly everyone was affected in one way or another by the Depression.

By 1933, 16 million Americans were out of work. They were frightened and angry, and their anger was easily directed toward minorities. Even before the Depression it had been difficult for Jews to become executives in some professions, particularly banking and insurance. Colleges had often refused to accept qualified Jewish students. During the Depression, these problems grew.

Brandeis University was ▶ established in 1948 to give equal opportunity not just to Jewish students but to students of all faiths. The three campus chapels symbolize the nonsectarian character of the university.

This photograph ▶
of the solarium in Philadelphia's Mount Sinai Hospital was taken in the 1930s.

It was especially difficult for Jews to gain acceptance at medical and law schools. And when Jews did graduate from medical school, it was difficult for them to find hospitals where they could work as interns. One reason was that so many hospitals were tied to Christian religious groups.

Jewish hospitals had been set up because many Jewish patients felt uncomfortable in these Christian hospitals. They could not get kosher food. They had to sleep in rooms which had Christian images on the walls. Now the Jewish hospitals became places where new Jewish doctors could practice their trade. In the same way, Jews who had studied law often set up their own Jewish law firms, independent of the established Protestant firms.

◀ *In his weekly radio programs of the 1930s and early 1940s, Father Charles E. Coughlin, a Catholic priest, advocated social and economic reform—and preached anti-Semitism.*

Henry "Hank" Greenberg was voted the Most Valuable Player in baseball in 1935 and again in 1940. Four times he led the American League in home runs and in runs batted in. But Hank Greenberg is perhaps better remembered for *not* playing baseball.

In 1932 the Detroit Tigers were in a tight pennant race. Concern was growing among the fans that if Greenberg did not play on Yom Kippur, the team's chances of winning the pennant might be hurt. When the Day of Atonement arrived, he refused to play, and the Tigers lost the game. But they went on to win the American League pennant that year, and Hank Greenberg had won the city of Detroit's respect.

Edgar Guest wrote this poem in honor of Greenberg:

Come Yom Kippur—holy fast day worldwide to the Jew—
and Hank Greenberg to his teaching and the old tradition true,
spent the day among his people and he didn't come to play.
Said Murphy to Mulrooney, "We shall lose the game today!
We shall miss him in the infield and shall miss him at the bat.
But he's true to his religion—and I honor him for that!"

In 1965 a Jewish major league pitcher also refused to play on Yom Kippur— this time at a World Series game. **Do you know his name?** (Sandy Koufax—the youngest player ever admitted to the Baseball Hall of Fame.)

Looking Ahead

Not just Jews but all minorities in America were suffering from a new prejudice. The fear of Communism and the belief that Jews and other minorities were "inferior" were spreading. For a while the Jews had been accepted in nearly every way, but now they were again being refused many of the rights they had fought so hard to win. This time the Jewish struggle for full equality in American society would include the Jewish struggle for the civil rights of blacks and women. As the movements for these three groups began to gather strength, everything was again interrupted, this time for a war, which was to change the Jewish world forever.

| 1933 | Hitler becomes chancellor of Germany. | 1941 | Germany declares war against the United States. | 1945 | World War II ends. |

Also in this chapter: The year an important Holocaust museum was opened. *Where is it?*

9 The Holocaust Years

German Jews ▶ were forced to buy yellow stars and sew them on all their clothing.

Across the ocean in Europe the Great Depression caused years of misery. In Germany, which had not recovered from the tremendous losses suffered after World War I, the Depression brought widespread hunger and unemployment. German banks closed, and the government grew weaker day by day.

During this time a man named Adolf Hitler became the head of a small political party. He preached that Germany had been betrayed by Communists and Jews. His National Socialist Party—the Nazi Party—rapidly gained popularity and within a few short years took complete control of the lives of the German people.

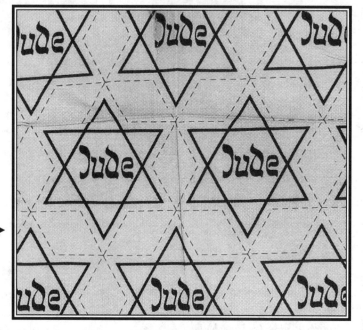

Holocaust **is a great fire that destroys all in its path. In Hebrew the Holocaust is called the** Shoah, **a word that means "a sudden collapse or devastation."**

New laws were passed that took away practically all the rights and possessions of the Jewish citizens of Germany. Jews were forbidden to serve in many professions. They lost their German citizenship. And they lost their right to attend schools and colleges.

World War II

The Nazis rebuilt the German army and air force, and in 1939 Hitler set out to conquer Europe. He was joined in this effort by the Fascist Party of Italy and later by the imperial Japanese. The Second World War had begun.

The large issue of the war seemed simple. All three of the major Axis powers—Germany, Italy, and Japan—were dictatorships ruled by powerful figures. The Allied powers—especially Britain, France, and the United States—championed the rights of peoples to form governments through majority vote. Most Americans saw World War II as a simple struggle of good against evil, freedom against dictatorship.

Nazi Anti-Semitism

For the Jews there was no escape from Nazi anti-Semitism. According to the Nazis, a person who was born a Jew—even a person who had only one Jewish grandparent—remained a Jew forever. The Jews of Germany had few choices open to them. The United States had placed strict limits on all immigration. Many other nations also closed their doors to Jews. Some Jews were able to find new homes in Britain and South America, but even these places refused to accept large numbers of Jews. Some managed to outrun the Nazis by moving east across Russia, as far as Shanghai and Australia, but most—fleeing to Holland, Belgium, and France—found themselves caught again when Germany conquered these countries.

The churches of Europe had always taught that the Jews were "strangers" and "nonbelievers." To escape the anti-Jewish teachings of the church, Jews had several choices: They could leave Europe for places like America. They could ignore the church and live in closely knit Jewish communities. Or they could either convert or pretend to convert to Christianity and just cease to be Jewish.

⬥ How was Nazi anti-Semitism different from the anti-Jewish teaching of the church?

⬥ Why was there no escape from Nazi anti-Semitism?

◀ *Many Jews tried to leave Germany. This photograph shows a crowd lined up in front of a Berlin travel agency that sold tickets to Palestine.*

▲ *In 1939 Felix Frankfurter was appointed to the U.S. Supreme Court by President Franklin Roosevelt. Though he and the president were close friends, they disagreed on how the United States should help the Jews of Europe. Frankfurter wanted the president to force Britain to open Palestine to all Jews fleeing Hitler, but Roosevelt refused to act. In the end Frankfurter was one of the many frustrated American Jewish leaders who could do little or nothing to help the Jews of Europe.*

The Final Solution

The Jews of Europe were trapped. Germany conquered the countries of Europe one by one, and the Nazis soon controlled the majority of the world's Jewish population. They began to discuss what they called the Final Solution to the Jewish question. They planned the utter destruction of the Jewish people, what we call the Holocaust.

The Nazis set up concentration camps and death camps to carry out the Final Solution. They built huge gas chambers in which to murder the Jews. Jews were rounded up in the ghettos and sent by train to the camps. There they went through a "selection"—some were sent immediately to their death in the gas chambers while others were used as slave laborers.

Those who managed to survive the Nazi concentration camps were barely alive when the war finally came to an end.

▲ *In the death camps, ovens were used to burn the bodies of Jews who had been murdered in the gas chambers.*

▲ *In 1944 a crowd
of 40,000 gathered
in New York City
in a demonstration
against the
Holocaust.*

Telling the World of the Slaughter

Rumors of the death camps spread to America, but these stories seemed too fantastic. Most people refused to believe they were possible. Few American Jews could accept the idea that our European Jewish relatives were being murdered in such an organized and cruel way.

Finally proof was produced—photographs, eyewitnesses, and written testimonies. American Jewish leaders like Rabbis Abba Hillel Silver of Cleveland and Stephen Wise of New York now tried to make the truth public. Most Americans were too concerned with the war effort to pay much attention. And most American Jews believed that if only the Germans could be defeated, the killing would stop.

Jewish leaders in America and Britain asked the Allies to rescue the Jews of Europe. They asked the Allies to bomb the railroad lines leading to the concentration camps. They even asked the Allies to bomb the concentration camps themselves. Despite the urgent pleas of the Jewish leaders, the Holocaust continued.

On October 6, 1943, one day before Yom Kippur, 500 Orthodox rabbis marched from the Capitol in Washington to the White House "to protest the silence of the world when an entire people is being murdered." President Roosevelt refused to meet with them.

Did American Jews Do All They Could?

Could the Jews of America have done more to save the Jews of Europe? Probably not. American Jews simply did not have enough power. They were afraid of anti-Semitism at home. They believed what the government told them, that the best way to help the Jews of Europe was to defeat the Nazis. They protested in public many times during the war years. They went to see the president and high officials many times. They organized committees of rescue many times. But nothing they did succeeded.

In the end money was sent to the Jews in Europe in the hope that some would be able to buy their way to freedom. The Zionists continued to press for a Jewish State in the Land of Israel. The Conservative and Reform movements spoke out against the mass murders but continued to believe that President Roosevelt was their best help.

When the war ended and the Nazis and their partners had been defeated, the world was shocked to learn the truth about the death camps. Six million Jews had been murdered! The word *genocide*° was used to define the slaughter. Yet even with all this proof, many American Jews found it difficult to believe the worst.

° **Genocide** is the intentional murder of a whole cultural group of human beings.

◄ *A 1944 poster to raise funds to help European Jews immigrate to the United States.*

The Holocaust survivors who came to America initially kept all but silent about the terrors they had experienced and witnessed. Few books were written about the Holocaust, and few testimonies or diaries were published from 1945 to the late 1950s. But times changed. Here are a few of the things that helped bring the Holocaust to the attention of the Jews of America.

In 1960 Adolf ▶ Eichmann, the Nazi most closely responsible for the death camps, was captured. His trial by the State of Israel was reported throughout the world and was even shown on television. The truth of the Holocaust was becoming widely known.

▲ The survivors realized they had to speak out or else never be heard, and writers like Elie Wiesel began to tell their own stories.

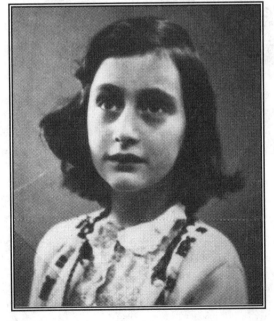

◀ The American Jewish author Meyer Levin discovered the diary of Anne Frank. It was made into a play and then a movie. Through her touching words this teenage German girl became the most famous victim of the Holocaust.

Looking Ahead

What happened in Europe in the Holocaust had a tremendous effect on the Jews of America. American Jews had lived through difficult years— years of anti-Jewish feeling and years of the Great Depression—yet these paled in comparison with the fate of the Jews of Europe. A thousand years of scholarship and Jewish life came to a sudden halt in the Holocaust as the largest Jewish community in the world was almost completely destroyed.

Before World War II the Jews of the world had always turned to the European Jews for leadership. Following the Holocaust the leadership of world Jewry fell to the Jews of the United States. Were the Jews of America prepared to accept this leadership? How would they respond?

▲ *By the 1990s American Jews, beginning to grasp the lessons of the Holocaust, established museums in many cities as permanent memorials to the victims of the Nazis. In 1993 the U.S. Holocaust Memorial Museum in Washington, D.C., a project of the U.S. government, was opened to the public. The museum is dedicated to presenting the history of the persecution and murder of 6 million Jews and millions of other victims of Nazi tyranny from 1933 to 1945.*

Also in this chapter: The year the first TV sets were sold. *Who was the man responsible?*

10 Opportunities and Challenges

◀ *Cemetery in France for American soldiers killed during World War II.*

At the end of World War II hundreds of thousands of soldiers returned home to America, many of them Jews. They were ready to build a new future, and America was ready for them.

World War II had lessened anti-Semitism in America. When the United States formally declared war on Japan and Germany on December 8 and 11, 1941, these countries became the enemies of *all* Americans, Jews and non-Jews alike. A new mutual respect could be seen in the way popular culture portrayed Jews. News reports, films, and novels emphasized the Jewish part in the American victory. In war movies the Jew was portrayed as smart, humorous, brave, and respected by his comrades.

Jews enjoyed great success in business. When *Forbes* magazine published a list of the 400 wealthiest Americans in the early 1980s, 25 percent were Jewish.

Anti-Semitism continued to decline after the war. Universities ended restrictions on the admission of Jewish students. Jews could now buy homes in areas previously off limits. Corporations hired more Jews, who now worked in high-level positions at such important companies as Bank of America, Chrysler, du Pont, Ford, and United Airlines.

The *Jazz Singer* featured a Jewish actor and singer named Al Jolson. The film tells the story of a cantor's son. His parents want him to become a cantor like his father, but young Jackie loves the popular music that his father hates. In a fit of rage his father throws him out of the house. Jackie rehearses for his opening night and dreams of success. But his opening performance turns out to be scheduled on Yom Kippur. Then Jackie's father becomes very ill and is unable to chant the High Holy Day prayers. In the end Jackie's love for his family and his religion is stronger than his love of jazz. He leaves the theater to return to the synagogue. The film ends as he chants the first prayer of the Yom Kippur service—*Kol Nidre*.

A New Industry

Before the First World War movie studios had made only silent pictures. Between World Wars I and II a technique was invented to join sound to motion pictures. The Warner brothers were the first to present actors speaking from the silver screen. Their first full-length talking picture, *The Jazz Singer*, became an instant success.

The film industry grew in Hollywood, and the Jews played a major role in shaping it. Movies became a very popular form of entertainment. Some Jews became movie actors, but most of the Jews of Hollywood succeeded as directors, producers, and screenwriters. The largest film studios—Paramount, Metro-Goldwyn-Mayer, Warner Brothers, and Twentieth Century Fox—were founded or run by Jewish businessmen.

▲ *In the beginning only a handful of Jews became movie actors. Among the best known were the Marx Brothers.*

THE FATHER OF TELEVISION

Of all the Jews who changed America, there is one whose work surely changed you! His name was David Sarnoff, and he came to the United States from Russia at the age of nine in 1900. In his teens Sarnoff became fascinated with a new invention called the "wireless," an early name for the radio. Before long he became a wireless operator at the American Marconi Company telegraph station in New York.

◄ *One lonely April night* in 1912, *as he sat at his desk, Sarnoff picked up a distress signal from a ship at sea. The* S.S. Titanic, *bound for New York on her first voyage, had struck an iceberg and was sinking! Sarnoff immediately notified the world through the wireless network, staying on duty for seventy-two hours to broadcast news of the disaster.*

Soon Sarnoff began to play with another invention—the "radio music box." He led the new Radio Corporation of America (RCA) and formed the National Broadcasting Company (NBC), the first radio network. In a short time nearly every home in America had a radio.

In World War II, Sarnoff helped organize a radio network to be used in the invasion of Europe by the Allies. The government thanked him by making him a brigadier general. But General Sarnoff wasn't through yet. He had another big idea—television.

Sarnoff's research led to the first television camera and the first television receiver. In 1946 RCA marketed its first television sets, and just twelve years later there were 180 TV stations in the United States.

▼ *By 1958 RCA had sold nearly 10 million television sets.*

Throughout his busy life David Sarnoff always made time to work for the Jewish community. He supported both the Educational Alliance in America and the Weizmann Institute of Science in Israel. He also served on the board of directors of the Jewish Theological Seminary for nearly twenty-five years. Sarnoff, known everywhere as the Father of American Television, died in 1971 at the age of eighty. His work had changed the world.

Success in Entertainment and the Arts

Many Jews became major stars in Hollywood, and people all over America knew them by name: Danny Kaye, Judy Holliday, Shelley Winters, Edward G. Robinson, Lee J. Cobb, and Kirk Douglas. Later they were joined by hundreds more. Names like Barbra Streisand, George Burns, and Steven Spielberg are household words today.

The Jewish tradition has always included music and musicians. Singers such as Richard Tucker and Jan Peerce often served as synagogue cantors before, during, and after their famous opera careers. Jewish composers like Richard Rodgers, Frederick Loewe, and Leonard Bernstein helped shape the American musical theater. A long tradition of Jewish fiddlers that began in Europe gave rise to some of the most talented violinists of modern America—Jascha Heifetz, Mischa Elman, Nathan Milstein, Isaac Stern, and others. In the arts Jews like the photographer Alfred Stieglitz, the painter Ben Shahn, and the sculptor Louise Nevelson also became famous.

Jews also gained success through their writings. The books and plays of Isaac Bashevis Singer, Herman Wouk, Arthur Miller, Lillian Hellman, Bernard Malamud, Neil Simon, and Saul Bellow were often based on Jewish issues but became popular among Jews and non-Jews alike.

If it sounds as though American Jewish life was just a list of names of people who succeeded, that is only so because so many Jews became famous in America that no single book could tell all their stories. We might even argue about whose story is most important to tell. Should we emphasize great legal minds like Louis D. Brandeis and Benjamin Cardozo; talk about a man like Bernard Baruch, who helped President Roosevelt bring the Depression in America to an end; or meet David B. Steinman, who built many of the world's greatest bridges? All of these people used their Jewish backgrounds and their great talents to make contributions to the American way of life.

Can you identify the people in these photographs?

(1. Richard Tucker; 2. Louise Nevelson; 3. I. B. Singer)

◀ *Nearly $1 billion was raised to build synagogues in the new suburban Jewish communities. This is Congregation B'nai Israel in Woonsocket, Rhode Island.*

From Cities to Suburbs

In the 1950s and 1960s American Jewish life was changing. Many Jews were moving out of the central cities to homes in the suburbs. Life was becoming more like the way it is today.

During this time 60 percent of America's Jews joined synagogues. Children continued to go to afternoon Hebrew schools and to Sunday schools. But despite the modern, comfortable buildings and high rate of synagogue membership, religious services were becoming less popular. Nonetheless, there were three times a year when almost all Jews came together. On Rosh Hashanah and Yom Kippur the synagogues were filled, and on Passover families sat around seder tables at home.

During the 1980s 75 percent of American Jews did not observe the Jewish dietary laws at home, 40 percent did not fast on Yom Kippur, and 90 percent did not attend a religious service once a month or more. One-third of American Jews had a non-Jewish spouse. *Are these statistics the normal result of living in a free society?*

Looking Ahead

How would the establishment of a Jewish state halfway around the world affect the great partnership of Jewish and American civilization?

Also in this chapter: The year a woman became prime minister of the State of Israel. *What was her name?*

A New State and a New Agenda

The last group ▶ of Jewish refugees finally left the displaced persons camps in February 1949.

In 1945 the Second World War came to an end. One-quarter of a million European Jews had survived the Holocaust. What would happen to them?

Some survivors tried to return to their homes, but the vast majority had no homes to go back to. A few went to search for family and friends. But most of these 250,000 Jews were placed in special displaced persons (DP) camps set up by the Allied Forces.

The conditions in these camps were terrible, and the survivors were desperate. After the war food was hard to find in all of Europe, and the displaced people in the camps were given very little. They lacked clothing and soap, linens and toothbrushes. They slept on bare boards and lived in cellars.

How would the American Jewish community respond to the needs of these refugees?

▼ *Jews born in Israel became known as Sabras—a name taken from the fruit of this cactus plant.*

Judah Touro left $60,000 in his will to be used to help the poor in the Land of Israel. ***Going back through this book, can you find other times when American Jews reached out to help the Jews of Eretz Yisrael?***

◀ *A ship called the* **Exodus,** *crammed with refugees, was captured by the British, and people all over the world were shocked when these Holocaust survivors were sent back to displaced persons camps in Germany. Do you think this was a good name for the ship? Why?*

The American Jewish Response

The Jews of America immediately organized to rescue the refugees. The Joint Distribution Committee sent money, clothing, and food—but it was far from enough. The Joint and other groups helped the survivors find the remaining members of their families and provided ships to help them escape from Europe. The Jews of Palestine provided most of the captains and crews. But where would the ships go?

American Jewish leaders worked with President Harry Truman to pass special immigration laws in 1948 and 1950 that allowed some 68,000 Jews to enter the United States. Altogether nearly 100,000 European Jews were permitted to enter the United States in the period just following the Holocaust. But even this was too small a number. Worse still, Great Britain, which controlled Palestine under the British mandate,❂ had promised its Arab allies that only a few Jews would be allowed into Palestine.

By 1947 nearly one-half of the Jewish population of Palestine was made up of Jews who had been smuggled into the country.

Thus began a strange chapter in world history. The Jewish communities of Palestine and America worked together to smuggle the survivors into the Land of Israel. The British tried to keep these boats from reaching shore. When they captured a boatload of Jews, they took the ship to Cyprus, where the Jews were put in detention camps. But despite the best efforts of the British, many boats did manage to reach Palestine.

❂ The **British mandate** was an order given by the League of Nations to England after the First World War to develop Palestine as a Jewish homeland.

▲ *Henrietta Szold*

Youth Aliyah helped Jewish children escape from Europe before and during World War II. The idea of taking Jewish youngsters from Germany to safety in Palestine was conceived by Recha Freier, the wife of a Berlin rabbi. The first group of Jewish young people was sent out in October 1932. A year later Henrietta Szold, an American woman, was made head of Youth Aliyah. By 1948, 30,000 children had been rescued from Germany and taken safely to Israel. Youth Aliyah continues its work today by training young immigrants for new jobs in Israel.

Henrietta Szold also founded Hadassah, an organization that operates a network of modern hospitals throughout Israel.

Reporters wrote about boats trapped by the British in the harbors of Palestine, and their stories became headline news around the world. In Britain, Jews spoke out against their own country's policies. In America, Jewish leaders demanded that the government of the United States protest the British blockade, and it did. The outcry against Britain became so widespread that the issue finally came before the newly formed United Nations. Finally the United Nations voted that the Jews be allowed to set up an independent state of their own.

On May 14, 1948, a declaration of independence was issued. The new State of Israel was established!

▼ *Chaim Weizmann, Israel's first president, presented President Truman (left) with a Torah scroll in thanks for U.S. recognition of the Jewish state.*

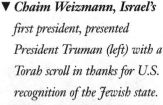

◄ *At the United Nations, Rabbi Abba Hillel Silver, leader of the American Zionist movement, argued for the establishment of a Jewish state in Palestine.*

American Jews and the Jews of Israel

Within hours of the birth of the new state, Israel was attacked by Arab armies on every border.

Thousands of Jews who had been imprisoned in the detention camps in Cyprus were now able to come to Israel. Many were given guns as they left their ships. They were joined by American Jews who traveled across the ocean to fight in the service of the new state. Somehow the Jewish soldiers—both trained and untrained—managed to stop the invasion. The Arabs withdrew, and the Jews of Israel began the work of building a new nation.

American Jews came to their aid. Hundreds of millions of dollars were raised in the United States to help the young state. At the same time American Jews called upon the government of the United States to support Israel with loans and foreign aid.

GOLDA MEIR

There was one Jew who understood the special relationship between America and the State of Israel in a way that no one else could. She was Golda Mabovitch, born in Russia in 1898. In 1906 her family settled in Milwaukee, Wisconsin, where Golda completed her education and became a teacher. She met and married Morris Myerson, and together they decided to live in the Land of Israel. In 1921 they traveled halfway around the world to their new home.

Seven years later Golda Meir began her political career. In 1946 she became the head of the Political Department of the Jewish Agency, and just before the State of Israel was declared, she was sent on a very successful fund-raising mission in the American Jewish community. Golda Meir continued her work in Israeli politics, serving as the first minister to Russia, as labor minister in the cabinet, and then as the Israeli foreign minister.

In 1969 Golda Meir, an American Jewish schoolteacher, became the first woman prime minister of the State of Israel.

One of the Americans who died in the Israeli War of Independence served as commander of the Jerusalem campaign to break the siege of the city. *Do you know his name?*

(Colonel David "Mickey" Marcus)

A Dangerous Mission

It was May 10, 1948. Everyone knew that the Arabs were preparing to attack. Golda Meir traveled by car into the very heart of Jordan, where she met with King Abdullah. She spoke of the need for Arabs and Jews to join together in peace, but the king said he could not keep his armies from attacking. Perhaps, he suggested, the Jews might decide not to declare their independence. Golda shook her head. That could never be. Nothing more could be said. Golda returned across the forbidden zone, back to Jerusalem. She would never set foot in an Arab country again.

When Dr. Martin Luther King, Jr. led a march for civil rights in Alabama, Rabbi Abraham Joshua Heschel (second from right) joined him.

The Kennedy Years

The finest moment for minorities in the United States came in the presidential election of 1960. Americans elected the first Catholic president, John F. Kennedy. The young president brought two children of Eastern European Jews—Arthur Goldberg and Abraham Ribicoff—into his cabinet. Jews of Eastern European ancestry had reached the inner circle of American government.

Life was continuing to improve for Jews in the 1960s. They used the judicial courts to gain the right to buy property in formerly "restricted" areas. They formed their own athletic and country clubs. Jewish plays, like *Fiddler on the Roof*, appeared on Broadway, and Hollywood began making movies, like *Goodbye Columbus*, that spoke openly of the Jewish situation in the United States.

Jews and the Civil Rights Movement

The Jews of America joined the struggle for civil rights. American Jews had been among the founders of the National Association for the Advancement of Colored People (NAACP) and were among the leaders of the civil rights movement in the South.

▼ *Arthur Goldberg became President Kennedy's secretary of labor. Later Goldberg was appointed a justice of the U.S. Supreme Court.*

Many Jews believe that fighting for the rights of all minorities in America ensures the rights of Jewish citizens. ***Do you agree? Why or why not?***

There was a price to pay. Jews in the South were scorned and attacked for helping the blacks. A few synagogues were bombed. Rabbis who spoke out against prejudice were threatened. Despite these actions, Jews continued to help blacks in the South and in the inner cities of the North, Midwest, and West.

The Kennedy years came to a violent end when the president was assassinated. Shortly thereafter the years of black-Jewish unity came to an end following the assassination of another important leader, the Reverend Martin Luther King, Jr. New black leaders pressured the Jews to resign their seats on the boards of black organizations and discouraged Jews from further involvement in the struggle for black civil rights. The violence of assassination was followed by inner city riots and was soon joined by an even greater violence that affected all of America.

Two Wars

The mid-1960s was a time of outright war—the war in Vietnam. Like many other Americans, many Jews opposed this war. In 1965 the Reform movement officially called for an end to the fighting, and a year later the Conservative movement joined in this call. In 1966 President Lyndon B. Johnson urged Jews to support the war in Vietnam as a way of repaying the president's support of the State of Israel, but Jewish organizations refused to connect these two issues. Rabbis and other Jewish leaders spoke out against the war, participated in anti-war rallies, and at the same time continued their support of Israel, seeing social justice in all their actions.

When Egypt threatened Israel's existence in May 1967, the Jews of America turned their attention away from the war in Vietnam to come to Israel's aid. They gave money, as usual, but this time they raised more money than ever before. By the hundreds American Jewish young people applied to go to Israel to fill civilian jobs so that Israelis would be able to fight.

What Do You Think?

American Jews have been accused of being as loyal to the State of Israel as they are to the United States. When asked which they would choose if there was ever a war between the two, many Jews said that such a situation could never come to pass.

✧ How would you answer the question?

◄ *Rabbi Jacob Rothschild made speeches urging integration and conducted seminars in his synagogue on civil rights. He is shown (right) in the ruins of The Temple in Atlanta, Georgia, after its bombing in 1958.*

By June 5, 1967, the day that war broke out in the Middle East, over 10,000 applications had been received from American Jewish volunteers. Some of them made it to Israel before the war began; many more waited at airports all over the United States.

It took only six days for Israel to win the war, yet the Six-Day War united American Jews in a way they had never been united before. There would be another war in 1973, when the Arabs would initiate an attack on the holy day of Yom Kippur. Again American Jews would rally to the side of Israel, and again Israel would manage to overcome the Arab armies massed against them. But 1967 was a turning point. Not since then has there been a time when so many of America's Jews were united in a single cause.

Israeli soldiers pray ▶
at the Western Wall after liberating the Old City of Jerusalem during the Six-Day War.

Looking Ahead

The Six-Day War changed the way American Jews behaved in American society. Israel proved that it was strong enough to defend itself, and the Jews of America were very proud. American Jews began to feel that they could also shape their own future.

Beyond this Jewish pride was another great discovery. America was now a country in which the opinions of minorities were respected and the minority vote was powerful. Jews spoke out on all the major social issues of the day. The battle for equality in the United States had been fairly won. America was not just a melting pot where minorities could become more "American" by becoming more like the Protestant majority. America was a complex jigsaw puzzle of cultures and civilizations fitting closely together to form a new whole.

12 Jewish Life in America Today

The Jews have always been a very small minority in the United States, and we continue to be a tiny percentage of the total American population today. During this study of history you have read about some of the many contributions that Jews have made to American society. These are all the more impressive when you consider our small numbers.

Today Jews continue to make great contributions—bringing Jewish values to almost every area of American life. We have proven that our civilization has much to offer our American nation. We are fortunate to live in a country where minorities can thrive and prosper, and we continue to discover that America's promise is even greater than we could ever have dreamed.

"Justice, justice you shall pursue. . . ."
(Deuteronomy 16:20)

The Jews of America have always faced the future by meeting the challenges of the present. In this final chapter we leave history and look ahead to the future. We will examine some of the challenges that face the American Jewish community today. But, as you will see, these are not only challenges but also opportunities—opportunities for us to build a better future as Americans and Jews.

◀ *You have read about several Jews who served on the U.S. Supreme Court. Do you remember their names? How many Jews are Supreme Court justices today?*

THE JEWISH POPULATION IN THE UNITED STATES (1993)

State	Estimated Jewish Population	Total Population	Estimated Jewish Percent of Total
Alabama	9,000	4,138,000	0.2
Alaska	2,400	587,000	0.4
Arizona	72,000	3,882,000	1.8
Arkansas	1,800	2,399,000	0.1
California	919,000	30,677,000	3.0
Colorado	51,000	3,470,000	1.5
Connecticut	97,500	3,281,000	3.0
Delaware	9,500	689,000	1.4
District of Columbia	25,500	589,000	4.3
Florida	622,000	13,488,000	4.6
Georgia	75,000	6,751,000	1.1
Hawaii	7,000	1,160,000	0.6
Idaho	500	1,067,000	—
Illinois	268,000	11,631,000	2.3
Indiana	17,500	5,662,000	0.3
Iowa	6,000	2,812,000	0.2
Kansas	14,000	2,523,000	0.6
Kentucky	11,500	3,766,000	0.3
Louisiana	16,500	4,287,000	0.4
Maine	8,000	1,235,000	0.6
Maryland	212,000	4,909,000	4.3
Massachusetts	270,000	5,998,000	4.5
Michigan	107,000	9,437,000	1.1
Minnesota	32,500	4,480,000	0.7
Mississippi	1,400	2,614,000	0.1
Missouri	61,500	5,193,000	1.2
Montana	500	824,000	0.1
Nebraska	7,000	1,606,000	0.4
Nevada	21,000	1,327,000	1.6

✧ On the chart, find the state you live in. What is the total population of your state?

✧ How many Jews live in your state? What is the Jewish percentage of the total population of your state?

✧ What is the total population of the United States?

✧ What is the Jewish percentage of the total U.S. population?

State	Estimated Jewish Population	Total Population	Estimated Jewish Percent of Total
New Hampshire	8,000	1,111,000	0.7
New Jersey	437,000	7,789,000	5.6
New Mexico	7,000	1,581,000	0.4
New York	1,640,000	18,119,000	9.1
North Carolina	20,000	6,843,000	0.3
North Dakota	600	636,000	0.1
Ohio	129,000	10,941,000	1.2
Oklahoma	5,500	3,212,000	0.2
Oregon	17,500	2,977,000	0.6
Pennsylvania	330,000	12,009,000	2.8
Rhode Island	16,000	1,005,000	1.6
South Carolina	9,000	3,603,000	0.3
South Dakota	350	711,000	—
Tennessee	17,500	5,024,000	0.4
Texas	109,000	17,658,000	0.6
Utah	3,500	1,813,000	0.2
Vermont	5,500	570,000	0.9
Virginia	68,500	6,377,000	1.1
Washington	33,000	5,136,000	0.6
West Virginia	2,500	1,812,000	0.1
Wisconsin	35,000	5,007,000	0.7
Wyoming	500	466,000	—
U.S. TOTAL	**5,840,000**	**255,082,000**	**2.3**

✧ Which three states have the largest Jewish population?

✧ Which state has the smallest Jewish population?

✧ Which state has the largest Jewish percentage of the total population?

The Aged in the Jewish Community

In the 1970s and 1980s a large part of the Jewish population was reaching retirement age and beyond. Older people often require special care. They suffer from the normal difficulties of age—loss of hearing and sight, the inability to walk without aid, and diseases such as Alzheimer's and cancer. The Jewish community has responded by building new facilities such as senior citizens' homes, cooperative housing for the aged, and nursing homes.

Within a few years the large number of Jews born just after World War II will become the largest group of Jewish senior citizens that the world has ever known.

◀ *Rabbinic students in California feed 200 homeless people every Monday throughout the year.*

This construction goes on in nearly every city in the United States. Some communities are also setting up Jewish hospices, a friendlier kind of hospital for those facing death. The problems of an aging Jewish community are just beginning.

"Honor your father and your mother." (Fifth Commandment)
"All who are hungry, let them come and eat." (Passover Haggadah)

The Jewish Poor

Beginning in the 1970s middle-class and well-to-do suburban Jews were discovering a growing number of poor Jewish Americans. Calling on a long tradition of *tzedakah*, the Jews of America banded together to form organizations to bring food to the homes of those who could not travel and to help those who were homeless. The Jewish poor continue to need help and support today.

Efforts to provide the ▶
special care that many older people require are an expression of Jewish values, including reverence for parents, respect for the aged, and a deep sense of the value of human life.

◀ *The first Conservative woman rabbi was ordained in 1985.*

Women and Judaism

Since the 1960s the place of women in Jewish religious life has been a vital concern for American Jews. By the late 1970s women were regularly being ordained as Reform and Reconstructionist rabbis and cantors and finding positions in synagogues. By the 1980s women were also becoming Conservative rabbis and cantors. In addition, women serve as synagogue presidents and hold nearly every other synagogue office.

Who Is a Jew?

Many American Jews choose to marry non-Jewish spouses. Sometimes these spouses convert to become Jews, but often they do not, even though the couple may choose to raise their children as Jews.

Traditional Jewish law claims that a child is Jewish only if the mother is Jewish. The Reform movement broke with tradition in the mid-1980s, and since that time all children who are born to at least one Jewish parent—either father or mother—have been considered Jews by the Reform movement if they are raised as Jews.

The question, Who is a Jew? is one of the most difficult facing the Jewish community today.

Other Special Concerns

Because of widespread divorce, many Jews between the ages of thirty and fifty have children but not spouses. The Jewish communities and synagogues provide clubs and sponsor events to help single parents find and support one another. Similar groups also try to help unmarried people.

Today a few Reform congregations have been established by homosexuals and are led by declared homosexual rabbis and cantors. The Jewish community's response to this issue continues to be a challenge.

▼ A serious effort is under way to foster Jewish continuity by encouraging families with young children to participate fully in Jewish life.

In the Former Soviet Union

The Jews of the former Soviet Union were the second largest Jewish community in the world, but they were treated as captives in the Communist world. They were forbidden to worship in synagogues, and they were discouraged from showing their Jewishness in any outward fashion. Yet the Soviet government refused to allow them to leave Russia. After the Six-Day War, Russian Jews became more active. They secretly organized adult study classes, taught themselves Hebrew and Jewish history, and applied for permission to immigrate to Israel or to the United States. The Communist government placed many Russian Jews in prison. They became heroes to the Jews of America and were called prisoners of conscience.

In 1989 and 1990 the Communist Party finally opened the doors of Russia. Russian Jews had been leaving in small groups since the 1970s, but now they left by the thousands. Using funds raised in the United States, Operation Exodus brought thousands of Jews to America and an astounding number—more than 500,000—to the State of Israel.

"Let the oppressed go free. . . ." (Isaiah, 58:6)

How will these new immigrants adjust to life in Israel and in America? And what about those Jews who continue to live in the former Soviet Union—will they renew their Jewish lives there, or will they choose to leave? How can we continue to help?

The State of Israel

The State of Israel has entered a new period in its history. Peace is being negotiated between old enemies—Israel and Egypt, Israel and Jordan, Israel and the Palestinians, Israel and Syria. New immigration to Israel continues, and it seems certain that the State of Israel will soon have as many as or more Jews than the American Jewish community. Peace and prosperity will certainly change Israel.

"Seek peace and pursue it." (Psalms 34:15)

How will the relationship between the Jews of America and the Jews of Israel change?

◀ *The search for peace between Israel and Jordan was begun by Prime Minister Yitzhak Rabin and King Hussein with the encouragement of President Bill Clinton.*

Looking Ahead

The next chapter in American Jewish history belongs to you. You will be writing it with your life. Years from now people will look back and ask what kind of person you were and what you did with your life that changed theirs—the same way we asked how our lives were changed by people like Haym Salomon, Ernestine Rose, Oscar Straus, Solomon Schechter, Isaac Mayer Wise, David Sarnoff, Golda Meir, and Louis D. Brandeis.

Our tradition places great importance on names. In the Talmud, Rabbi Simeon ben Yohai says:

There are three crowns—the crown of Torah, the crown of the priest, and the crown of the ruler—but the crown of a good name is greater than all of them. (Avot 4:13)

The question of American Jewish history, the one that remains for you to answer, is ***Where will your good name appear?***

Index

Hillman, Sidney, 57
Hillquit, Morris, 55
Hitler, Adolf, 68
Holliday, Judy, 78
Holocaust, 80
Holocaust Museum, 74
Homosexuality, 91
Hospices, 90
Houston, Jewish settlement in, 31
Hussein, King, 93

I

Immigration Laws, changing, 63
Inquisition, 9
International Ladies Garment
    Workers Union (ILGWU), 56, 57
Isabella, Queen of Spain, 10
Israel (Eretz Yisrael)
    Arab opposition to, 83
    establishment of, 82
    farming in, 37
    helping Jews in, 34
    and peace negotiations, 93
    Six–Day War in, 85–86, 92

J

Jacksonville, Florida, Jewish settlement
    in, 31
Jacob's Staff, 10
Jastrow, Marcus, 23
Jazz Singer, 76
Jefferson, Thomas, 28
Jewish Agency, 83
Jewish charities, organizing, 50
Jewish community, aged in the, 89–90
Jewish Community Center (JCC)
    movement, 52
Jewish Daily Forward, 53, 57
Jewish dietary laws, 79
Jewish family names, 30
Jewish Institute of Religion, 59
Jewish poor, 90
Jewish population, in the United
    States, 88–89
Jewish Record, 24
Jewish rights, fight for, 14, 47
Jewish Theological Seminary (JTS),
    23, 46, 77
Jews
    Ashkenazic, 17
    Crypto, 9
    first, in America, 9–14
    German, 21, 34, 35, 42, 45, 68–69
    immigration of, 17, 39–42
    Russian, 36–37, 42, 55, 63, 92
    Sephardic, 20, 28
Johnson, Lyndon B., 85
Joint Distribution Committee, 49,
    52, 81
Jolson, Al, 76
Jonas, Charles H., 24
Jonas, Edward, 24
Josephs, Jacob, 45

K

Kaplan, Mordecai M., 52
Kashrut, 22
Kaye, Danny, 78
Kehillah, 48
Kennedy, John F., 84–85
Kern, Jerome, 43
Key West, Jewish settlement in, 31
King, Martin Luther, Jr., 85
Kohut, Alexander, 23
Ku Klux Klan, 48

L

Labor movement, 53–60
Lazarus, Emma, 38
League of Nations, 81
Leeser, Isaac, 23
Lemlich, Clara, 55
Leonard, Benny, 43
Levin, Meyer, 73
Levy, Asser, 13
Levy, Uriah Phillips, 32
Levy brothers, 29
Liberty Bell, 15
Lincoln, Abraham, 24, 25, 26
Lithuania, Vilna, 45
Loewe, Frederick, 78
Lopez, Aaron, 20
Louisiana Purchase, 28

M

Macy, R. H., and Company, 33
Maimonides, 51
Malamud, Bernard, 78
Marconi Company, 77
Marcus, Josephine Sarah, 30
Marshall, Louis, 47, 48
Matzah, 16
May Laws, 36
Medicine, Jewish contributions to, 61,
    62
Meir, Golda, 83, 93
Menauhant Hotel, 47
Metro-Goldwyn-Mayer, 76
Miami, Jewish settlement in, 31
Michelson, Albert Abraham, 61
Miller, Arthur, 78
Milstein, Nathan, 78
Minhag America (The American
    Ritual), 22
Minuit, Peter, 12
Mitzvah, 42
Morais, Sabata, 23
Morris, Robert, 18
Mostel, Zero, 43
Myerson, Morris, 83

N

National Association for the
    Advancement of Colored People
    (NAACP), 59, 84
National Broadcasting Company
    (NBC), 77
National Catholic Welfare
    Conference, 63
National Council for Soviet Jewry, 92
National Council of Jewish Women,
    42
National Socialist (Nazi) Party, 68, 69,
    72
Netanya, 34
Nevelson, Louise, 78
New Amsterdam, Jewish settlement in,
    11–13
New Orleans, Jewish settlement in, 21
Newport, Rhode Island, Jewish
    settlement in, 16, 17, 29
New York City
    attempt at self-government in, 48
    Eastern European Jews in, 40–41
    federations in, 50
    garment trade in, 53
    Jewish settlement in, 17
Nineteenth Amendment, 26
Noah, Mordecai Manuel, 30
Nobel Prize, 62

O

Ochs, Adolph, 48
Old Testament, 15
Operation Exodus, 92
Organization for Rehabilitation
    through Training (ORT), 49, 52

P

Paramount, 76
Passover, 16, 27
Pasteur, Louis, 34
Peddler, 33
Peerce, Jan, 78
People of the Book, 15
Pescadero and San Mateo Stage
    Company, 29
Philadelphia
    Jewish settlement in, 17
    Mount Sinai Hospital in, 66
Phoenix, 30
Pittsburgh, Jewish settlement in, 21
Pogrom, 36
Polio, 62
Protocols of the Elders of Zion, 47
Purim Ball, 27

R

Rabbinical Council of America, 45
Rabin, Prime Minister, 93
Rabinovitz, Sholem, 38
Radio Corporation of America
    (RCA), 77
Recife, Brazilian colony of, 13
Reconstructionist Foundation, 52
Reconstructionist Magazine, 52
Reform Judaism, 22, 23, 60, 72, 85, 91
Rhode Island, 16
Ribicoff, Abraham, 84
Robinson, Edward G., 78